The HERO Method for Small Businesses

The HERO Method for Small Businesses

The Surprising Truth about Facts vs.
Feelings — Communication Secrets that
Increase Response and Revenue

Kathryn Gillett

© 2017 Kathryn Gillett
All rights reserved.

ISBN: 1976247802
ISBN 13: 9781976247804
Library of Congress Control Number: 2017914556
CreateSpace Independent Publishing Platform
North Charleston, South Carolina

Also by Kathryn Gillett

The HERO Method for Tech Companies

The Journey: a Novel

To Linda and Mari —

The HERO Method — and this book — took the dramatic trajectories they did thanks in huge part to your unwavering support. I am forever grateful.

WHAT THEY'RE SAYING ABOUT THE HERO METHOD

Global 100 Organizations
Amazon

> "I rely on Kathryn and The HERO Method to create customer-centric messaging and storytelling that will generate more reach, engagement, and response."
> — Sr. Category and Marketing Leader, AWS Marketplace

Dell

> "Using The HERO Method, Kathryn found unique messaging that positioned us as a true value-added Solutions Provider — which meant we no longer had to sell on price-point alone."
> — Global Value-add Software Solutions Program Manager

Microsoft

> *"The HERO Method took us out of the 'business as usual' communications rut we were in, and guided us to award-winning storytelling."*
> — DIRECTOR OF PRODUCT MANAGEMENT, SQL SERVER GROUP,

Small & Medium-sized Businesses

> *"Thanks to The HERO Method, our year-over-year growth increased from 33% to more than 62%!"*
> —VP SALES SOLUTIONS, UNIVERSAL MANAGEMENT SOLUTIONS

> *"Kathryn and The HERO Method helped us win 2012 Microsoft Partner of the Year award! We could not have done it without her!"*
> — VICE PRESIDENT, U.S., SPECIALIST SOFTWARE SERVICES.

> *"The HERO Method transcends 'state of the art' business communications. It is a breakthrough methodology for creating truly compelling content by cracking the code about the real power of story."*
> — CLIENT DEVELOPMENT DIRECTOR, R2INTEGRATED - DIGITAL MARKETING AGENCY

WHAT THEY'RE SAYING ABOUT THE

"The HERO Method is on the forefront of management trends."
— PRESIDENT, *EXCLAIM!*

"The HERO Method is not just another way to communicate your message to the market. It is a powerful way to communicate your vision. The HERO Method gets underneath all the features and benefits, and uncovers the attitude shift the audience goes through to get to 'Yes.' Because of that understanding, we have found more meaningful proof points to support that shift."
— VP MARKETING, *AGILE ADVANTAGE*

"The stakes were really high for us, and Kathryn's HERO methodology brought a fresh approach to our messaging. She created messaging that helped our prospects visualize the value our company would bring them — and feel the reward we would deliver in the end. The HERO Method cuts through the clutter, captures the audience's attention, and tells our story in a compelling way."
— VICE PRESIDENT U.S., *SPECIALIST SOFTWARE SERVICES*

"The HERO Method is nothing short of visionary. It allowed us to get to clear, compelling, human messaging

and content that we never would have arrived at in a hundred years!"
— CEO, UNIVERSAL MANAGEMENT SOLUTIONS

"The world would be a better place if all marketing and sellers followed this path."
— Founder, Selling to Zebras

"The HERO Method gets inside of what drives a brand. It helped us stop, reflect and understand the key components of who we are, why people buy from us, and what our essential messaging should be."
— VICE PRESIDENT, MILLIGAN EVENTS

Solo-Preneurs

"It took me 10 years to build a list of 45,000. Then, using The HERO Method, it took me two weeks to attract 73,000!"
— FOUNDER, SOCIAL ENTREPRENEUR EMPOWERMENT NETWORK

"Once a year we do a series of webinars that provide free training and enroll new clients in our paid program. Before working with Kathryn, our previous largest launch had been $400,000. After working with Kathryn on messaging, we came away

with compelling core concepts and powerful language that capture the essence of our solution, who it's for, and the immense value people can receive. We sent out emails using The HERO Method messaging that offered the same webinar series with the same paid program offer as before. The results included attracting 73,000 attendees from at least 50 countries and over $700,000 in sales — nearly twice the response and revenue we'd achieved before. Your messaging is critical to your tangible results, and The HERO Method can help with both."
— FOUNDER, VISIONARY BUSINESS SCHOOL

"The HERO Method made a huge impact on my businesses! My results have been fantastic because our messages are so much more powerful! I'm receiving calls from new clients every week thanks to The HERO Method. I routinely hear this from new clients: Just by reading my website, they knew they wanted to work with me. I know this sudden change is because my communications now address THEIR needs in a simple, authentic, and honest way."
— PRINCIPAL, MARIN COUNTY NOTARY

"Thanks to The HERO Method, my website lets me engage potential clients in discussions more easily, with greater impact, and in far

more interesting ways. Since my new website has been up and running, I have had many important prospective clients and potential partners tell me how useful it was to have explored my website. They continually tell me how attracted they were to my offerings because of what they learned there."
— LEADERSHIP SHERPA

"I'm sitting here creating new copy for my website and am so full of gratitude for The HERO Method! Everyone should have such an angel in their life! The HERO Method messaging hits the right notes so cleanly. And makes creating copy a joy!"
—PRINCIPAL, MARIN COUNTY NOTARY

"The HERO Method gave us a new view into our products and customers. The process is simple, yet powerful. As a startup, we were uncertain as to how to best explain what we do and how that's of value to our market. The HERO Method helped us pinpoint compelling marketing messages that we never would have arrived at on our own."
— FOUNDER, SNUGGLEPAC

"I had thought the branding and website design process was going to be an onerous one. But with The HERO Method, the process was easy, enjoyable, and energizing. In the

WHAT THEY'RE SAYING ABOUT THE

end, I found the process to be illuminating! I learned more about the true nature of my work, the value it carries in the world, and the impact that my services have. Even after building my career over 30 years, I am newly energized to bring my offerings into the world with greater clarity, passion, and impact."
— PRINCIPAL, RETRIEVER ADVISORS

"The HERO Method gave me the freedom to not TRY to be a 'marketing person,' but to communicate in a way that truly expresses who I am. It gave me permission to express my authentic passion about my products and services."
— JEWELRY MAKER AND ARTIST

DISCLAIMER

This book is designed to provide information about a new approach to creating more effective business communications. It is sold with the understanding that the publisher and author are not engaged in rendering legal consulting services.

The purpose of this book is to explain The HERO Method. In doing so, the author intended to complement, amplify, and supplement previous research and texts on related topics. You are encouraged to read other sources of information, learn as much as possible about business communications, and tailor that combined information to your individual needs. A starting point for your research could be the Bibliography at the back of this book.

This is not a get-rich-quick book. Increasing response rates from business communications takes discipline and a methodical approach to improvement.

Every effort has been made to make this manual as complete and as accurate as possible. However, there may be mistakes, both typographical and in content. Therefore, this text should be used only as a general guide and not the ultimate source for creating effective business communications. Furthermore, this book contains information on business communications that is current only up to the printing date.

The purpose of this manual is to educate and entertain. The author and Sunne Publishing shall have neither liability nor responsibility to any person or entity with respect to any loss of damage caused, or alleged to have been caused, directly or indirectly, by the information contained in this book.

If you do not wish to be bound by the above, you may return this book to the publisher for a full refund.

CONTENTS

	This is where we begin............ xxi
Part I —	**A New Mindset with New Possibilities** 1
	Introduction 3
Chapter 1	Mindset Shift #1 — H2H, not B2B 7
Chapter 2	Mindset Shift #2 — Connecting, not Selling 17
Chapter 3	Mindset Shift #3 — H2H, not Jargon ... 25
Chapter 4	Mindset Shift #4 — It's your Sales Pipeline, but it's their Decision Journey 33

Part II —	**How to SHIFT INTO This New Mindset.**	**39**
	Introduction	41
Chapter 5	H — Human-to-Human Communication	43
Chapter 6	E — Emotional Connections: I feel, therefore I buy	51
Chapter 7	R — Relevant Information: It's your Sales Funnel, but it's their Decision Journey	67
Part III —	**How to APPLY This New Mindset In Creating Connections**	**97**
	Introduction	99
Chapter 8	Motifs of Transformation	105
Chapter 9	Archetypes of Transformation	113
Chapter 10	Metaphors	117
Chapter 11	Creating the Output — Websites	125
Chapter 12	Creating the Output — Sales Support Tools	139

Chapter 13	Creating the Output — Social Media · 155
Chapter 14	Creating the Output — What About Facts? · · · · · · · · · · · · · · · · · 161
Chapter 15	Creating the Output — Now It's Your Turn · 165
	Epilogue · 169
	With Gratitude. · · · · · · · · · · · · · · · · · · · 171
	Author's Notes · · · · · · · · · · · · · · · · · · · 173
	Bibliography. · 175
	About the Author · · · · · · · · · · · · · · · · · 183

THIS IS WHERE WE BEGIN...

Do you remember the story of the frog who's in a pot of water and he can't tell that the water is gradually heating up? (Spoiler alert: this version of the story will have a *happy* ending.)

Like that proverbial frog, small business communicators are sitting in the same warm water that we have been for years. The problem is: the water is heating up. What actually generates sales seems to be out of our control. Our messages aren't standing out from the increasingly congested crowd. Audiences seem indifferent to our content. Response rates are dismal. And our successes are based more on hit or miss than know-how.

I get it. I'm intimately familiar with the waters of this pot. I started hopping around in it 25 years ago. From the first moment I plopped into it, I was trained to figure out the features, advantages, and benefits of a product or service. I was trained to look for creative, "out of the box" ways to say the same things in different ways. I "knew" that being clever was what got attention. And getting attention was the most important thing.

But about 10 years ago, the water I'd been so comfortable plopping around in started heating up. I noticed that it didn't always work to create content and programs based on those accepted assumptions. Doing it the way "everyone knows it should be done" didn't always result in higher response rates and revenue. It started to dawn on me that this approach was too hit or miss. I'd been trained as an experimental psychologist in college (I was pretty good at it, too — in my junior year, a scientific journal accepted an experiment I had conducted). The scientific method I'd learned in college told me that if these "tried and true" techniques worked, they should work every time. Or at least most of the time. But they don't. The fact is, most business communications isn't measured. Because it's not measurable.

Trying to find a helpful pattern, I often looked at advertising awareness rates and compared them to sales rates. But that data never plotted out to anything close to a 1:1 correlation. There was no statistical relationship between people remembering an ad and buying the product featured in it. I was frustrated because I could see the problem, but I had no idea what to do about it. So I stayed in the water, flopping around, even though it was starting to feel warmer than I would have preferred.

THIS IS WHERE WE BEGIN...

Then I wrote a novel.

And everything changed.

I had been an avid student of Joseph Campbell's work from the moment I first saw the PBS series, "The Power of Myth." Campbell was a world-renowned anthropologist, specializing in world mythology. His studies of the ancient motifs of story famously coalesced into what he called "The Hero's Journey" — a pattern of storytelling that has been told throughout human history. (I did some of my own research on this subject and concluded that hundreds of the most famous stories that have come to us across time and culture have these same mythic motifs at work.)

At the same time, I was an amateur Elizabethan historian, reading history books for fun. (I was such a history nerd that for 25 years, I never read one work of fiction.)

One fateful day, I decided to write a historical fiction novel. I laid out the mythic motifs of The Hero's Journey as the "skeleton" of the story and then fleshed out those bones with the actual events of Francis Drake's circumnavigation of the globe. The result was an award-winning novel that readers describe as "a page turner." (If you're interested, it's called *The Journey* — and it's available on Amazon.)

That's when the water really started heating up for me. I began to think, "if I could take the dry facts of history and bring them to life using these mythic motifs, what if I could do that with business communications? The more research I did on how the human brain works — and how these mythic motifs instantly lock into our unconscious mind, the hotter the water got. I had to admit to feeling that I'd been wasting my clients' time and money using communication techniques that just didn't work anymore. (If they ever really did.) The more research I did on marketing results the more it became clear that being clever had nothing to do with sales success. That talking about features and advantages and benefits was turning people away instead of persuading them to buy. I could deny it no longer: our accepted business communications paradigm was broken beyond repair.

So I hopped out of the pot and created The HERO Method.

The most important aspect of The HERO Method is that it's a new paradigm about creating content that connects to our audience's unconscious minds. Yes, the end result is higher response and revenue. But the path to get there is by creating authentic, human-to-human connections.

What we'll be exploring here is powerful stuff — we're reaching into people's unconscious minds. And, like The Force in Star Wars, there is a Dark Side potential to this new paradigm: Its power can be — and has been — used to manipulate people. But The HERO Method is dedicated to only using this force to help make our audience's world a better place. By keeping that goal in mind, our messaging is more compelling, our content is more persuasive, and our results are increased response and revenue.

THIS IS WHERE WE BEGIN...

Here's the logic of it: People buy stuff that helps make their life better; they buy stuff that helps make their world a better place. If you show your audience how you can make their world a better place, people will buy more of your stuff.

Based on the results I've seen, this hypothesis is proving to be true. It's been used to create content of all kinds — from websites and customer stories, to slide presentations and product demos. It's been used by some of the biggest names — and some of the best "behind the scenes" small businesses— in the world.

Using The HERO Method, I've garnered response rates in the double digits for lead generation and relationship marketing programs. The HERO Method creates clear and connecting messaging that clients swear they "never could have arrived at in a hundred years." It has created content and websites that have helped clients break through to new levels of sales. It has helped other clients win coveted international awards that were strategic wins for their business growth.

Remember that proverbial frog in the water? Here's the good news: Scientists have proven that frogs are perfectly capable of sensing the water warming up — and always jump out of the pot long before they're damaged in any way.

So, what I'm here to say is: it's time to jump out of the water of the "communications as usual" pot. There's a whole wide world out there of better ways to achieve the results you're looking for. I wrote this book to help you find your own unique path to get there.

In Part I of this book, we'll explore the "outside the pot" world that is The HERO Method. We'll discuss four mindset shifts that are involved in following The HERO Method so we can get the results we want.

In Part II, what you'll find is that The HERO Method is like putting on 3-D glasses: by changing the way we look at business communications, we can change the results we get.

Then, in Part III, we'll dive into how to APPLY this new mindset shift to your communications. This is where we'll explore the power of The Ancient Bones of Story in creating "unconscious content" — content that directly and instantly connects with your audience's unconscious mind.

Which is exactly what we need to do so we can all be happy frogs, freely exploring new ways to create compelling content that gets the results we want and need.

PART I

A NEW MINDSET WITH NEW POSSIBILITIES

PART I

INTRODUCTION

> *"You ARE passionate, Mozart.*
> *But you do not PERSUADE."*
> – Emperor Joseph II, "Amadeus"

Maybe what we think is true, isn't true

Squatting on top of a termite mound, David Greybeard was "fishing for insects." He had stripped a straight twig of all its leaves and inserted the denuded twig into the termite mound. Termites inside the mound bit into the twig, so when David pulled it out, he could insert the twig into his mouth and snack on his yummy treats.

Unbeknownst to David, Jane Goodall was observing his behavior from a discreet distance.

You've probably figured out that David was not human. Dr. Goodall had named this chimpanzee David, as well as the other chimps she observed exhibiting similar behaviors.

What Dr. Goodall observed meant that physical anthropology books had to be re-written. She had observed chimps modifying objects to make tools. Until that time, scientists were certain that only humans used and made tools. In fact, our species was defined as "Man the Tool Maker." "Everyone knew" that tool-making is what separated humans from other animals.

Since that now-famous day in October, 1960, researchers have observed a number of other animals using tools. Even reptiles are now among the tool-makers in our world. (Alligators and crocodiles have been observed layering small sticks on top of their snouts to attract birds looking for nesting materials!)

The point is this: It can be the very thing that we're sure is true that turns out to not be true after all.

I believe that business and marketing communications is ready for a similar shift in mindset.

Until now, business communications has been about keeping a professional distance from our audience. Business schools teach how to analyze marketing results, but not how to create compelling emotional connections. We have vehemently insisted that "Business-to Business" (B2B) is very different than "Business to Consumer" (B2C) communications. We see example after examples of complex concepts like, "Application Programming Interface," getting turned into an acronym (API). The assumption is that an acronym is going to make the *concept* easier to understand. (It doesn't.) We liberally douse our content with words we believe are impressive, like *optimize* and *maximize*. We've been told time and again that our product or service is the hero and that every page of our content should have a "hero shot." Our overall strategy is based on sell, sell, selling to people by pushing and pulling them through our sales funnels.

This is the mindset that needs to be shifted.

And the first assumption we need to shift to is the fact that every buy is an emotional buy. Period.

Why your audience's reaction to emotional content is more important than all the facts you can throw at them

Amanda's heart races as she lowers herself onto the narrow CT Scanner table. A motor hums as the table draws her into the belly of the scanner. She is told to lie very still. She is told to hold her breath. She closes her eyes. And in 30 seconds it's all over. There have been hundreds of scenes like this — hundreds of men and women who have been pulled into CT scanners — not to save their lives, but to understand how visual, verbal, and written communication works in the human brain.

These studies are the rationale behind what I'll share with you throughout this book.

The HERO Method isn't just a new-fangled idea. It's firmly rooted in neurology and psychology and sociology and anthropology. It's based on decades of research, including state of the art fMRI research on how the living brain responds to stimulus.

Scientific studies prove that we are hardwired to be drawn towards authentic, human connections.[39] And that reaching out to our audience from that place, rather than from the place of "professional objectivity," is where real persuasion happens.

What we'll see in Part I, is that by turning our existing assumptions on their head, we can move into a new realm of possibilities for breaking through, standing out, and generating measurable improvements in response and revenue.

CHAPTER 1

MINDSET SHIFT #1 — H2H, NOT B2B

> *"...selling isn't some grim accommodation to a brutal marketplace culture. It's something we can do better by being more human."*
> — DANIEL H. PINK, "TO SELL IS HUMAN"

I'LL NEVER FORGET my first writing gig. It was back in the olden days of technology— the Heady '80s — when every software application was new and different. To us, the challenge wasn't how to differentiate our solution — it was how to build credibility and trust. To accomplish this, writers like me were directed to write in a specific tone. It was believed that techno-folks would feel manipulated by emotion, so only a tone of emotionally-distant professionalism could possibly develop credibility. The same thing was happening in every area of business. There was "business speak" and "at home speak" and ne'er the twain shall meet. As time passed, business writers tried to inject enthusiasm while steering clear of emotion. Thus evolved the menagerie of hyperbolic words we use today —maximize, optimize, and market leader.

The business world has evolved its own way of communicating to its audiences. The rule is to adopt an objective, detached tone — sprinkled with accepted business-speak words.

But what if this emperor isn't wearing any clothes?

The fact is, audiences are increasingly skeptical about what they're reading. Advertising has lost its credibility, and everyone recoils whenever there's a hint that someone is "trying to sell us something."

I saw an ad recently on YouTube that had a series of inspiring stories of people, some of them famous, who had achieved what others said they couldn't. It was high production quality — a very expensive ad. The stories were engaging and had believable emotional impact. I stayed with it out of curiosity to see what the product was going to be and how the advertiser was going to tie their "solution" into these emotionally inspiring stories. The product? Not a non-profit educational fund or a graduate school that helped these celebrities overcome adversity. It was a credit card. A credit card. Really? I was so mortified at the manipulation that the ad still has a negative impact on me as I now edit these words months later.

MINDSET SHIFT #1

This speaks to the need to create emotionally engaging content *that doesn't trigger our audience's balderdash detectors*. We need to draw our audiences closer to us. We've got to stop boring them with business jargon and acronyms — and stop trying to manipulate them with hyperbole. We need to "talk" to them, human being to human being. We need to share information in a way that's quick and easy for them to understand. And paint clear pictures in their minds about how our solutions help make their world a better place.

To be human is to have emotion. And emotion drives decisions.

This may be ancient history to you personally, but I want to talk about Apple's "Think Different" ad campaign. Each ad featured portraits of famous people — from the Dalai Lama to Albert Einstein to John Lennon. The only other elements on the page were Apple's logo and two words: Think Different. It ran from 1997 to 2002. That kind of run may happen often on Broadway, but not in the ad world. Then add to that the fact that most of us still easily remember the 15-year-old campaign. That certainly attests to its "sticking" power.

So, why were these ads so successful? Yes, they featured portraits of famous people, but so have lots of short-run campaigns. The difference is that these ads connected with us emotionally. By featuring world-famous change-makers (not just famous "pretty" people), each ad communicated deeply-felt beliefs that resonated with "the rest of us."

This is what we all need to do — create emotionally compelling connections that resonate deeply with our audience as human beings.

But the problem is, we in the business world have inherited the philosophy of, "He who has the most information wins." Our websites are chock full of pages and pages of content that inundate our audience with facts and more facts about our solutions.

Here's the dilemma: although we know that the purpose of a website is to persuade, emotion is what persuades, not facts. What science has proven, and continues to prove over and over again, is that emotion, not reason, is the power behind our decisions to act. Basically, every buy is an emotional buy, no matter how "rational" we think our audience is.[14, 44]

Let's say you're shopping for a car. You need a practical car for your growing family. You're doing your due diligence, searching the web for your options. You're searching for safety and fuel efficiency and enough room for your kids, their friends, and all their soccer gear. So far, this information — these facts and data — are mostly being processed in the neo-cortex. This is where analysis takes place.

Then, you see a minivan that looks really cool — you wouldn't be embarrassed to drive this car. And, it has leather seats! You call your spouse over to check it out. The

MINDSET SHIFT #1

reaction isn't what you hoped it would be...until you read out that it also has a built-in vacuum and theatre-quality rear-seat entertainment. You both decide right then and there to go take a test drive.

My bet? You're going to end up buying that car.

What's happened is that the limbic brain has kicked in. This is where all of our *emotions* are rooted. It's the part of our brain that knows whether something is important to us or not. It's also where we learn, and remember — and it's where we are motivated to take action.

As brilliant as our rational brain is, it's got a huge handicap compared to the emotional brain. The rational brain is a sluggish turtle compared to the cheetah-fast limbic brain. The limbic brain zips out messages at 40,000 bits of information per second, but the neo cortex sloshes along at only 40 bits per second.

So, once your limbic brain is engaged, your rational mind is a goner.

In the end: *reasoning does not drive behavior*. It's the emotional, limbic brain that initiates the human "call to action". (In fact, decisions cannot be made without the limbic brain. People who have sustained damage to their limbic brain are incapable of making decisions.)[37]

What we've done in the business-to-business world is to assume that our content needs to be fundamentally different than content that's directed to consumers. But no business ever bought from another business. And the term "consumer" is another marketing construct that dehumanizes the audience. Let's face it, the very same person who "consumes" their favorite soda — and shuns all other sugary, carbonated beverages — is the same person who's wondering whether or not you're the right choice for them. That's why The HERO Method sees all business communications as creating human-to-human (H2H) connections.

We have been taught by our marketing predecessors — and are constantly reminded by the status quo — that to convince people to choose us over the other guys, we need to talk about the most powerful features of our products and services. But there is absolutely no research to support that assumption.

The truth of the matter is that even the engineer-iest engineer makes decisions based on emotion, not on fact. When it comes to intellect versus emotion, our brains are hardwired to give emotions the upper hand.

Revenue-generating proof that H2H authenticity works

A tested example of the shift we're looking at comes from Patagonia, the innovators of high-tech outdoor equipment and clothing. Patagonia continues to report record revenues and profit using a very human approach to marketing.

MINDSET SHIFT #1

Patagonia's founder is Yvon Chouinard. In his inspiring book, "Let My People Go Surfing," he says:

"Our catalog is our bible for each selling season. Every other medium we use builds from the catalog's editorial standards."

And what are those standards?

"Patagonia's is a human voice. It expresses the joy of people who are passionate about their beliefs and who want to influence the future. It is not processed, and it won't compromise its humanity."

Does this uncompromising humanity work? It sure does.

I use this example because catalogs are highly measurable. Literally every inch is measured for effectiveness. The current catalog wisdom is: the more space you use to sell stuff, the more you'll sell. Patagonia has always broken that rule. Amazingly, they use a full 45% of their space to tell customers' stories about how they relied on Patagonia's clothing and equipment. And what has happened whenever they've reduced the story content and used more catalog space to sell product? Click-through and sales have dropped![20]

Rather than trying to be impressive, we need to get laser-focused on what's really important: our audience needs to *easily* understand *how our solution will make their life better*. We need to ask these questions every time we create content:

- Is this content easy for our audience to read and understand?

- Is it clearly saying what's important to our audience?

And, most importantly:

- Does it help the audience see themselves experiencing our solution?

You may be thinking, "Patagonia is selling to consumers. I'm selling to businesses." But that doesn't matter. A human being who is a "consumer" over the weekend is the same human being at work during the week. When it comes to building credibility and trust with any audience, what works is human-to-human (H2H) content. That's because the receiver of our content is never a business (or a "consumer"); it's always a human being.

MINDSET SHIFT #1

TRY THIS:

> *"The emotional system exerts the first force on our thinking and behavior."*
> — GERALD ZALTMAN, "HOW CUSTOMERS THINK"

The science is irrefutable; to be persuasive, to increase response and revenue, we have to connect to the limbic brain of our audience. Period.

But the accepted tone of business content is impersonal and objective. That means it disconnects rather than connects us to our audience. Now's the time to shift our mindset and start reaching out with authentic human connections.

No matter what you're selling, your audience is— regardless of their job title or role in life — very human.

1. Go to your homepage and honestly assess how much your company uses a "professional," dispassionate tone. How often do jargon and acronyms show up?

2. Content that never compromises its humanity has been proven to work.[20] Changing your mindset doesn't take a revolution. Evolution will work just fine. Again, try taking an honest look at your home page and consider how you can increase the "humanness" of the experience your audience has when they land on your site. Even if you don't change anything on the page, this exercise could be an illuminating lesson for whatever new content you create.

CHAPTER 2

MINDSET SHIFT #2 — CONNECTING, NOT SELLING

When I was growing up, my extended family would get together for holidays at my Aunt and Uncle's house. My Uncle, may he rest in peace, would always participate in discussions with his philosophy of, *The Louder You Are, The Righter You Are.*

We've got to be honest about this: we've all been guilty of this in our communications.

Our headlines shout out what we think is most important about our solution. And our content regales our audience with the details of our solution — how much better and faster and cheaper it is. Of course we have every right to be proud of our solutions. But that excitement too often ends up being expressed in a way that bores our audience with the details of how it all works — and why that's better than the competition.

Maybe this is why our products and services aren't selling better.

Instead of trying to sell, sell, sell to a bunch of anonymous "someones," we need to shift to connecting with our audience from an authentic place. When we reach out consistently on a human-to-human level, we'll build more balanced and trusting relationships. If we do this, even in a sea of competition, we can stand out and attract people who are more likely to buy.

In Chapter 1, we began exploring the importance of the limbic brain as the seat of emotion and decision-making. The limbic brain is also where we learn, and remember, and develop loyalty, and are motivated to take action.

We're all familiar with the fight, flight, and freeze response to stimulus. But what we're not so familiar with is that there are more subtle impulses in the brain that affect our behavior pretty much all day long. Let's say you love chocolate, and you hate carrots. When you see a piece of cake and you think it's chocolate cake, your brain sends out chemicals that, in neurological terms, "draw you toward it." But when you learn that it's carrot cake, your brain sends out chemicals that draw you away from it. Every single time we see something we feel positive about, our brains draw us toward it. Whenever something strikes us as unpleasant, our brains move us away from it.

This makes perfect sense in terms of evolutionary survival. The brain is a pattern-recognition machine that is designed to predict what's going to happen next. Those who can react faster to stuff that can poison or kill them, are the ones who are more likely to survive.

Research also shows that *our brains re-create the emotions we "see" in what we read.* When we read a novel, we literally experience the same feelings that the character is feeling. Our brains light up in the same areas as if the events were actually happening to us. We are hardwired for connection — even in what we read.

This is essential for us to grasp because we're creating the "drawing toward or away from" response every time our audiences read our content. We're either creating connection or we're not. Our content has concepts and visuals and words that either draw people to us or away from us. And your audience would not be able to tell you why; it's all unconscious.

The content we create has to connect positively with our audiences' limbic brain so they will feel drawn toward us. It's that simple. And that complex: We have to carefully craft every word and visual of our content so our audience will feel drawn towards us as they experience our content.

Connection and memory

Of course, when we create content, we want people to feel interested and curious enough to read it. But we also want them to remember it. If they don't buy right away, we want them to remember our key messages and to have a positive association with our company a week later, when they're deeper into their decision-making process.

All of the sights, sounds, and content your audience are "drawn toward" are also going to have a profound effect on their ability to remember what they've read.

Neuroscientists are in complete agreement: Your audience cannot remember what they've read without having an emotional (limbic) connection while they're reading it.[14, 23]

I can't say this more emphatically: *All of the facts in the world cannot overcome a negative emotional reaction to our content.* What's worse is, if the facts cause confusion or overwhelm, the facts themselves will create unconscious negative emotional reactions and neurological resistance to what you're saying.[54]

How connecting helps you stand out

People are hardwired for connection. And your audience is yearning for you to *talk to them like a human being*. If your communications genuinely connect with your audience, right there, you're standing out in a huge way. You're shouting from the mountain top that you genuinely want to connect with them in an authentic way. I'll bet none of your competition is doing that.

MINDSET SHIFT #2

How connecting helps you attract

Quite simply, connecting feels better than being sold. People will feel drawn toward you when you authentically — even if imperfectly — try to connect with them. And they'll feel drawn away from you when you try to sell them.

How connecting affects buying behavior

People do business with people they know, like and trust. If you continue to authentically reach out to them, they will continue to be attracted to you throughout their decision-making process. Of course, they will be more likely to buy from you!

TRY THIS:

People do business with people they know, like, and trust. And nobody likes to be sold to. Every word and color and visual element in your content has a powerful effect on the unconscious reactions in your audiences (we'll explore this in detail in Parts II and III).

Unconscious emotional reactions are what draw people toward you or away from you. Scientists have proven that creating even the most subtle negative emotions causes people to "back away" from the source of that unpleasant emotion.

That, right there, explains a lot about why our bounce rates are so high.

To stand out from our competition, reduce bounce rates, increase response, and cultivate sales, we need to shift our focus from coaxing to connecting.

1. Again, go to your website. Try looking for these signs. These are the top reasons that cause your audience to feel resistant about connecting with you.

    - Is your content focusing on facts?

    - Is it in *any way* confusing or frustrating?

    - Is it coming off as inauthentic?

    - Is it trying to SELL them?

MINDSET SHIFT #2

2. Look honestly at how you're using your communications to try to sell, sell, sell. Then make a commitment to create content that authentically connects with your audience about how your solutions help change their world.

CHAPTER 3

MINDSET SHIFT #3 — H2H, NOT JARGON

> *We work on behalf of our clients offering the most comprehensive and structured range of consultancy services in the framework of a long term strategic partnership in order to optimize ROI through realistic TCO reduction.*

How MANY TIMES did you have to read that to understand what it meant? And, even when you figured it out, were you able to *imagine yourself benefiting from their solution?*

In the business world — and in business schools — we're taught that keeping a cool distance is a way to gain respect. That if we're too "friendly" people will question our expertise. That aloofness equals taking things seriously. That authentic human passion and excitement is unprofessional.

There are a number of problems with this, as we've already seen. But in this chapter, we're focusing on jargon.

Have you ever left a note to yourself somewhere because you want to remember to do something every day? Have you noticed how it doesn't take long before you stop noticing the note? That's called habituation. All humans do it. Basically, your brain says, "I've seen the thing once or twice, maybe three times. I don't need to notice it anymore."

I believe that's what's happening with our dispassionate, jargon-rich content. Because we're trying so hard to be taken seriously, we create words and phrases like "best practices," and "driving business success." But our audience has habituated to those words. Which means their brains are literally not paying any attention to them. Their eyes are scanning the words, but their mind is wandering somewhere else more interesting. Take the words, "innovative solutions." Can you see how those words have completely lost their meaning from overuse?

Here's another example. Back in the day, there were five personal computers on the market. Apple II, Commodore Pet, IMSAI 8080, MITS Altair 8800, and Radio Shack TRS-80. Which name is the simplest, most human (most relatable)? We know what happened to all the rest.

The solution sounds simple, but is difficult to do because our beliefs about what sounds "professional" are so entrenched. The fact remains that what we need to do is create content with a H2H quality that seems more like a real conversation.

A friend of mine works in the legal field. He is hired by lawyers to create videos that show juries "a day in the life" of victims of serious accidents. These people are often paraplegics and quadriplegics as a result of a car accident. His job is challenging in that he needs his videos to generate compassion for the challenges the person and their family deal with every day. But the judge will throw out the video if she feels it's manipulative.

This is very much what we are tasked to do.

Reason doesn't work like a judge who objectively weighs evidence. It works more like the lawyer whose job is to persuade the jury to award the settlement amount he feels is deserved.

Researchers in this field all agree — and I can't make this point often enough: *If you want to persuade people, you have to appeal to their emotions.* Content filled with jargon, and told in a professional tone will, quite literally, turn readers off.[10, 17, 44, 62]

But what about the facts?

Of course, the rational mind is involved in decision-making. But information takes second place to connection. Emotion is the first-string player. Information comes in **after the fact**, bolstering the decision to take action. People quickly reach conclusions based on emotional reactions, then find facts later to support what they've decided.[17, 44, 58]

Let's take buying a car. We may think we make perfectly rational decisions around buying our cars. But it's easy to see that buying a car is not a *rational decision* — otherwise we would all be driving the same car — the one that is the safest and has the best gas mileage.

So, here's what happens. You make a choice based on aspects of the car that make you feel good; that "draw you toward it." THEN you gather up all the facts about the car to support that emotional reaction. And that's how we make big decisions.

Basically, we quickly (at 40,000 bits a second) reach conclusions based on our emotional reactions, and produce reasons later to justify what we've decided.

We see this all the time in politics — on both sides of the isle: A perfectly intelligent person saying the most idiotic thing…and really believing it.

When it comes to our content, yes, information is important. But only after we have created a positive emotional response.

This is a powerful thing to realize. And we can use it to make deep and authentic connections with our audience…. or send them running for the hills.

Be careful how you use facts

Think about the times you have gone to a website and felt frustrated because you can't find an answer to even the most basic question. The other day, I went to my bank's website

MINDSET SHIFT #3

to make an electronic transfer. Couldn't do it. Could NOT find a way to do it. Now that's just silly.

Not wanting to frustrate our visitors is a no-brainer. But research shows that even a small amount of uncertainty generates a negative response in the brain.

When most of us go to a new website, the most common experience is to find it difficult to get a basic understanding of what the business does and what they have to offer. How many times has that happened to you? It's frustrating, right?

Those pages are filled with facts. Facts that are causing you to bounce out of their site.

What if that's happening on your site? What if your facts and insider jargon are creating uncertainty? If that's what's happening, your audience's brain will trigger a sensation of physical distress that's so subtle they're not conscious of it. (Remember the "drawing towards or away from" discussion in the previous chapter?) If your site is creating the *slightest* negative emotional response, your audience is unconsciously "shifting in their seat." The brain is telling their nervous system to get ready to withdraw. If content is confusing or frustrating, their body starts receiving stress hormones — long before they're conscious of it. That means "before they know it", they're bouncing out of your site — with no positive association of the experience, and no memory of what they've read.[26]

This will also happen if your content triggers their "balderdash detectors." In trying to express how great our solutions are, we tend to fall back on hyperbole. We're "the best," we're "the fastest," we're "the first." But if our audience doesn't believe what we're saying, their brain will start "calling the retreat." The same thing will happen if they feel they're being sold to. (We all like to buy — but nobody likes to be sold.)

So, stand out from your competition by sharing your genuine enthusiasm for the topics you're discussing. Avoid reader resistance by avoiding insider jargon. And "talk" to them as if you were in a compelling conversation with them. That's the kind of content that sparks interest…gets read…and develops relationships.

TRY THIS:

Next time you create new content, try creating it based on a topic that your audience is curious about or needs to know. That's what will create the essential first step: emotional connection.

Then don't blow it by using an aloof, "professional" tone or insider jargon. Instead, create content with a H2H quality that seems more like a real conversation. You'll stand out from your competition with content that's easy to read and information that's easy to understand…and that won't create the unconscious neurological resistance that causes bounce.

1. Imagine you're talking to a prospect at a social gathering. Tape record yourself talking about the topic. Notice how you explain these concepts in Real Human Language (RHL — *just kidding*). Transcribe that into the first draft of your content and see what you come up with.

2. The business-speak words we've been using for years, like maximize, optimize, and market leader no longer have any meaning to our audience. Go to your homepage and count how many times you see:

    - enable

    - maximize

- optimize
- leverage
- anything close to "the first, best, or fastest.'

Now consider finding other words to express those concepts.

CHAPTER 4

MINDSET SHIFT #4 — IT'S YOUR SALES PIPELINE, BUT IT'S THEIR DECISION JOURNEY

We've been trained in the business world to think of the sales process as a "pipeline." We "pull" prospects into our pipeline, and "push" them through the pipeline until they become customers.

But if we stay focused on the audience's perspective, it's easy to realize that they don't see it that way. They have a problem, they're looking for a solution, and they need to make a decision about which solution is best for them.

So, instead of a sales pipeline (which is the last thing they'd want to be in), let's see them as being in the process of making a decision — a Decision Journey. We'll be diving deeper into how to connect with your audience as they move through their Decision Journey in Part II. But for now, let's just talk about it from a big picture perspective.

The Decision Journey is the process your audience goes through in order to make a decision. At the beginning, they're stuck in a situation, then they start looking for other ways of doing things, they weigh their options, then they make a decision.

Pretty obvious, right? But the question is: how do we stay connected with them as they transition through this process? If we're only looking at pushing and pulling them, we'll miss the mark. We'll be communicating with them based on our own agenda, instead of connecting with them based on where they are in their Decision Journey. By identifying with them based on where they are in THEIR process, we can humanly and authentically stay connected with them.

Who's the Real Hero?

We've also been "raised" to perceive our solution as The Hero. But that's another mindset shift we need to make. Why? Because that's another reason our marketing isn't working as well as it could…as well as it needs to.

Think about it this way: when we're focused on telling our audience how great our "hero" is, our content ends up sounding chest-beatingly self-absorbed. "Look at us and what we do and what we've got and how fast we do it!"

MINDSET SHIFT #4

That's no way to start and keep a relationship.

In this new mindset, The Hero is your audience. This is a big mindset shift, but it's an important one. When we take the spotlight off ourselves and turn around 180-degrees, we can see that The Hero is our audience who's on The Quest for a solution to what's ailing their company or their life.

Your audience is mired in a problem, and their perception about how things are done keeps them stuck there. Whether your content is an email, a slide presentation, web content, video, or product demo, its role is to do more than help an audience **understand** your solution. Your content must inspire them to **want** your solution. To do that, we must transform their point of view — from doing and seeing things "their old way" to seeing how much better their life will be if they do things "your new way".

How do we do that? By giving them helpful insight and advice that *honors and supports their process of transformation*. That's the way to help them move themselves forward through Their Decision Journey. (This is the essential role of "Mentor" — a powerful force for change that we'll dive deeper into in Parts II and III.)

Too much information can paralyze The Hero and end The Quest

Another aspect of this mindset shift is to realize that we're all guilty of inundating our audience with information and options. Remember how emotion beats information when it comes to persuasion? While a little information can help support the emotional decision to act, too much information is like kryptonite to Superman. Decades of research shows that having a few options to choose from can be helpful in encouraging people to buy. But having too many choices — and too much information — impairs decision-making. What's the most common response to too much information? No purchase decision at all.[54]

This is another reason why all of the content we're pushing out to our audience may actually be **causing** our bounce rates.

On the other hand — again based on research — if you make their Decision Journey easy, prospects are far more likely to choose your solution…and are even more likely to recommend you to others![54]

MINDSET SHIFT #4

TRY THIS:

To recap: Your audience is The Hero who is on a Decision Journey to solve an important problem. And your solution is The Treasure they seek.

1. We'll dive into more specifics in Part II, but for now, think about how your audience is on Their Quest for a solution. Try on a mindset that envisions your audience as The Hero on a Quest. From that mindset, you'll see new ways to create content that supports your audience's mental process of transformation — from only knowing The Old Way, to seeing how great it could be to do it Your New Way. If you're the source they trust in gently creating that mental transformation, they're much more likely to respond to your content and choose your solution. For now, just try that concept on for size. Whenever the topic of "our audience" or "our solution" comes up, think about them in these terms. We'll dive into the particulars later.

PART II

HOW TO SHIFT INTO THIS NEW MINDSET

PART II

INTRODUCTION

So far, we've explored the mindset shifts (and the science behind them) that we need to embrace in order to create content that gets the results we really want and need.

In Part II, we're going to put on 3-D glasses to look at business communications from a new perspective. We need to shift the way we perceive the purpose of business communications. If we don't, we'll continue to create content the way we always have — and we'll continue to get the same lackluster results.

This is where "the coin will drop" for you about the title of this book — and the name of this methodology. The letters H, E, R, and O represent the foundation of The HERO Method's approach to creating content. The "H" stands for human-to-human communication, the "E" for emotional connections, the "R" for relevant information, and the "O" for valuable output.

The first three letters refer to the shift in perspective that we need to make in order to create unconscious, persuasive connections. We need to look out at the world of business communications from this new "3-D" perspective. If we don't, our Output — the content we create — won't be any different than before. That's why we'll explore the H and the E and the R in Part II. Then we'll dive into the details around creating the "O" in Part III.

Get ready for the first leap out of the proverbial pot. I hope you find being out here as exhilarating as I do.

CHAPTER 5

H — HUMAN-TO-HUMAN COMMUNICATION

> *"Our charter is to inspire and educate rather than promote."*
> — YVON CHOINARD, FOUNDER OF PATAGONIA.

IMAGINE WALKING INTO a party. You glance around the room. No one you know has arrived yet. You walk over to the snacks table and, as you load up your plate, you start chatting with a guy who's also digging in to the vegies and hummus. Instead of an engaging conversation, he talks about himself and is preoccupied with success and getting ahead. He disregards your feelings; it's almost as if you're not there. Pretty soon, you realize that you don't quite trust everything he's saying. Just then, a friend arrives and with relief you leave him to his self-involvement to go talk to a person you can relate to and trust. That person you were just talking to was exhibiting symptoms of "narcissistic personality disorder."

Unfortunately, there is a similar disconnect in a lot of the small business marketing content out there. In our well-intended enthusiasm to show how our solution is the hero for our prospects and customers, we can end up sounding narcissistically self-absorbed and indifferent to our audience.

Yet again, we're not to blame. This is how we've been trained. The content strategies that have become the business world's stock-in-trade are leaving audiences feeling disconnected and stage-managed. In doing everything we can to get our audience to open our emails and click on our links, we risk undermining trust and connection. In Chapter 1, we talked about the importance of shifting to an authentic, human tone in our content. In this chapter, we're going to dive deeper into content strategies that generate more sales by engaging more people.

The science of human-to-human (H2H) connection

One of the proofs that we're hardwired for H2H connection is a psychological phenomenon called *reciprocal affinity*. Here's how it works: when we receive a "gift" from someone — even a stranger — our brains are wired to respond with a "gift" in return.[17, 62]

HUMAN-TO-HUMAN

We've all received mail from charities that have a small gift inside — return address labels, a pen, or ornamental flags. Why? Because it works. Regardless of whether or not you have personally responded to such mailings, the carefully-measured results prove their worth. When mailings are accompanied by small gifts, they produce far higher donations. That's why scientists also call this behavior *reciprocal altruism*, because often the value of the money given in return is far greater than the value of the gift that was received.

In a similar vein, social scientists know that social relationships are built when people do things out of a spirit of generosity — without an expectation of getting something in return.

The same is true with economic transactions.

In the consumer world, "reciprocal affinity" is a well-known principle of good marketing. It basically means that when you give something to your customers, they're more likely to do business with you. The more you give, the more they'll buy. We see this all the time in grocery stores: free samples of products. Global brands all around us use it: from Disney to McDonald's, Starbucks to Apple, Nike to Nordstrom.

This speaks to the importance of offering "freemiums" — free "samples" of our solution as a first step in the relationship-building process. There's no doubt in my mind that it's a proven approach that all companies can benefit from.

H2H not SELL

This is a tough one for a lot of people — shifting away from selling to connecting. But, just like any bad habit, it's worth a little willpower and discipline to break it.

The fact is nobody wants to be sold. When your audience is looking for a solution, the minute they get so much as a whiff that you're trying to sell them something, they've emotionally withdrawn before they're even conscious of it. And the more you continue to SELL them, the more likely you'll lose them altogether.

So, what can we do?
1. **New Mind Set.** Rather than focusing on sales pitches and enticing offers, think about creating content that will turn you into a trusted partner. It may be hard to stop aiming at immediate sales, but if you have anything other than an impulse purchase to offer, you can truncate your sales cycle by proving that you're a trusted resource when it's time for them to make their purchase decision. When prospects trust you, there are lots of other benefits: lower price sensitivity, higher margins, more repeat business.

2. **Patagonia is a proven example to follow.** The founder himself, Yvon Choinard eloquently expressed the importance of H2H communications in his book, "Let My People Go Surfing":

"Patagonia's image is a human voice. It expresses the joy of people who love the world, who are passionate about their beliefs, and who want to influence the future. It is not processed; it won't compromise its humanity. This means that it will offend, and it will inspire."

"As for style, we write as though we were the customers. We don't speak to what is perceived as the lowest common denominator. We speak to each customer as we want to be treated, as an engaged, intelligent, trusted individual."

We talked about Patagonia in an earlier chapter, but I want to make it clear that theirs is a catalog business. That means, literally every inch of their content is measured and analyzed. And whenever they have experimented with giving more space to "sell" stuff, the result has been that customers end up buying less. (Again, I highly recommend reading … no, *studying*, Choinard's book.)

Remember:

- No business ever bought from another business. "Consumers" are as unreal as avatars in a video game. No matter what their role is in society, the people who need what you have to offer are human.

- <u>Always</u> begin <u>every</u> communication with a human connection.

- Always write in an authentic, human tone.

TRY THIS:

Over the past years, I have reviewed the web content of well over 100 small business websites. Without exception, the content was primarily about the company and not about their audience. But that's actually good news. If everyone out there is doing this, then your company can stand out from your competition by using your content to create meaningful, human connections with your audience. Here are some concepts to contemplate. (We'll dive into the details of creating content in Part III. So, for now, just let these ideas roll around in your head.)

Websites: Think of your website as an ambassador of your company. Is it receiving your readers the way you would want a human to receive them in person? We tend to be generous at trade shows…but not on our websites.

"About Us" content: Do you express your authentic passion about the subject? Do you stay focused on how the information is valuable to the reader?

Blog Posts, Social Media: Does your point of view provoke discussions around ideas that are relevant to customers and that move them emotionally?

CHAPTER 6

E — EMOTIONAL CONNECTIONS: I FEEL, THEREFORE I BUY

> *"If it weren't for our emotions, reason wouldn't exist at all."*
> — Jonah Lehrer, neuroscience writer

IMAGINE YOU'RE IN an upscale department store. You see a pair of gorgeous Italian shoes. And you think, *Ooh, I would love to wear those.* (OR, if you're really honest, *I would love to be seen wearing those.*) What's happened is that dopamine has subtly flushed your brain with pleasure. Even though you're fully aware that you do not need the shoes, in the time it takes for your heart to beat about three times, you've made your purchase decision but you hear yourself saying, "I'll just try them on…" After you've tucked the credit card receipt into your wallet, the dopamine-induced euphoria subsides, and doubts about the wisdom of that purchase seep in. We often call that buyer's remorse.

But no worries, you've got your rational brain at the ready. And what does it do? It generously gives you all kinds of "rational" reasons to support your completely irrational purchase decision. Satisfied that you've made a completely logical decision, you begin preparing the speech to convince your spouse of what a perfect purchase it was. (My favorite has been, "Look how much money I saved!")

Using fMRI analyses, neuroscientists agree this is the basic decision-making process that takes place in every fully-functioning human mind. The people who buy your products and services are all human beings. And all human beings buy because they think the product or service will somehow improve the quality of their life.

Don't believe me yet?

Let's take a well-known case of "John" a man in his 30s who sustained a brain injury in a car accident. By the time the accident happened, John had risen to the top of his profession as a financial analyst. After the accident, IQ tests showed that John was as intelligent as before. He could still crunch the numbers with the best of them. He could still read the most complex data and make sense of it.

The tragedy of the accident is that he can no longer make even the most basic decision.

Why? Because John's brain injury has left him unable to feel emotion. It would be natural to assume that being emotion-free would be an advantage in decision-making. John could make fully rational decisions, like Mr. Spock's Vulcan side — free from those pesky, irrational emotions. But unlike Vulcans, John is human. And without emotion, every option feels neutral. He feels no preferences for anything. He has no way to sense which option is best.

John's sad story has played out time and again for people under scientific scrutiny who have sustained damage to the same part of their brain. Every one of them were fully capable of making complex decisions until neurological damage to the limbic brain caused them to lose access to their emotions — and simultaneously lose their ability to make decisions.[37]

Decision-making is not a rational process

This is what researchers have proven over and over again. If it was, we'd all be living in homes with the same architectural design — a design that's affordable and efficient at keeping us warm in winter and cool in summer. We'd all be wearing the same functional clothes. And expensive Italian shoes — or high-status watches — would have no appeal...unless their expense was related to being perfectly functional.

What tricks us into thinking we're rational decision-makers is what happens after we have the emotional reaction to the item we are drawn toward. After we've made our emotion-based decision, the rational brain kicks in and comes up with all kinds of reasons to support the emotional response…regardless of how irrational those reasons actually are. We see this all the time in television interviews when otherwise intelligent people say the most inane things, then go on to defend what they said for equally inane reasons.

This is why we think we're so logical. Because of the list of reasons we collect to support our decisions. When in fact, the basis for the decision is purely emotional.

Trust — The Human Glue of Connection

Emotions are important, but trust is essential.

I hope I've made it clear that emotions are essential for decision-making. And, since most of us want our audience to at least put us on their short list when they first encounter our solution, I hope it's clear that we need to immediately generate emotional connections with them.

But which emotions? The primal emotions we want their brains to feel are: "This feels good." "I am safe." "This company (or concept) is not a threat to me."

In other words, we want them to feel *trust*.

But from the very first connection, you're up against a powerful emotion of resistance. It's the defense against "being sold." The opposite of trust. Whether you're reaching out to them in an email or a phone call, or they're visiting your website, at some level, your audience is in a state of resistance, thinking, "They'd better not try to get me to do what I don't want to do."

We need to be keenly aware of this — and counter it with a more powerful emotion.

There are lots of positive emotions that humans feel. One is happiness. A commonly-held theory in advertising is that making an audience laugh will influence them to buy. But research does not support that. Turns out, just being entertained does not cause us to remember anything. It does not cause us to take action. But we see exactly that in ads all the time. All I can say is somebody is wasting a lot of money on those ads.

The emotion we generate needs to connect our audience to us in a way that's meaningful *to them*. The best way I know how to do that is by building the emotion of trust.

Stephen Denning, the author of "The Secret Language of Leadership," was one of the first to speak to this point in detail. He talks about how the deliberate shading of the truth can have devastating effects on trust and credibility. And how that in turn has devastating effects on the business. "Even an apparent lack of openness," he says, "can be disastrous."

This is an essential point that we need to be ruthlessly honest with ourselves about: We need to constantly ask ourselves this: Are we guilty of this? Do we let our focus on the competition, our focus on bringing in new prospects, our focus on meeting the quarterly projections, leave us in a mindset that convinces us that it's OK to stretch the truth in the name of "making the sale?"

We need to be vigilant in remembering where the money really is: smack dab in our audience's hand. And for them to let go of it, for them to gladly give it to us, they need to trust us. And for them to trust us, truthfulness is crucial.

From sales-pitching to trust-building

Imagine landing on a website that spotlights an apology for a huge mistake the company made. Then, on another site, you see they've highlighted an offer that trusts you to pay whatever you feel their offer is worth. That's just crazy, right? Not really. There is plenty of proof out there that trust is not just good for one-on-one relationships, it's also good for business.

Here are two examples.

- The rock band Radiohead was the first to release an album online and trust fans to decide how much to pay for it. The band generated more revenue for that one album than for all its previous releases.

- The University of Michigan Health System (UMHS) risked legal liability by encouraging its doctors to apologize when they made mistakes. Trusting that patients would be forgiving paid off for UMHS. The number of malpractice suits fell, so much so that other providers are taking the same approach.

These examples show how building trust with our audience can be an act of courage. Well... a series of them, really. Yet it can quickly pay huge dividends. In addition to the reward of good will that everyone feels (or maybe because of them), building trust can reap higher response rates, loyalty, and revenue.

When you win a prospect's trust, you earn more than just the first sale. When customers trust your company, they are more likely to become return customers — even enthusiasts who gladly recruit new customers.

Negative Emotions

Since the top advertising and marketing agencies so often use negative emotions, it's easy to assume that these multi-million-dollar ads get results. Let's look closer at that hypothesis.

Anxiety and Fear

In 2001, BMW created a series of short films called, "The Hire." These were not your typical feel-good commercials, showing a happy family touring mountain roads in their comfy car. These movies were intense mini-thrillers that evoked lots of fear and anxiety. In their first four months, the series earned more than 11 million views— and BMW sales shot up more than 12 percent.

On first blush, one could conclude that anxiety and fear are what worked. But there are a number of other variables at play here. First, Clive Owen is the star, and — with very little dialogue — he created an intriguing "James Bond meets Rambo" kind of hero. The scripts were written by top Hollywood writers, and directed by icons like Ang Lee. The result was a series of riveting short stories. Yes, they're thrilling, yes, they made me feel anxiety and fear, BUT each one ends on a very positive note. The Hire always saves the day, using his super-human driving skills in his invincible BMW that continues to perform automobile acrobatics despite sustaining viscous damage. In other words, these are mini success stories where the hero uses a BMW to save the day. They're really a series of the classic "lone hero on his trusty steed" motif. After each episode, we are left with a positive feeling about how The Hire (which is interestingly close to The Hero) saved the day — and couldn't have done it without his BMW.

Compare this to the "Mayhem" series of ads from Allstate. If you're not familiar with the series, actor Dean Winters brilliantly portrays "Mayhem" — the force that can cause big trouble for home and car owners: A teenage driver. A raccoon in the attic. An inaccurate GPS system.

According to Advertising Age, in 2011, Mayhem was in third place as the most-recognized advertising character, behind Geico's gecko and Progressive Insurance's Flo. (In touting success, most ad agencies stop there. They call it "recognition.") But research showed that the gecko and Flo were both accurately tied to their respective companies over 90% of the time. (That's more important than just recognizing the character.) But for Mayhem, only 41% of consumers surveyed were able to link Mayhem with Allstate. That's not good.

But the real test of marketing is the bottom line: and the results of these fear-based (and expensive) ads were stagnant revenue for Allstate.

Scientists explored this idea for GM and Nationwide. As volunteers viewed two fear-based commercials, fMRI scans revealed a noticeable amount of stimulation in their amygdalas, the region of the brain that generates dread, anxiety, and the fight-or-flight impulse.

In other words, these multi-million-dollar commercials were literally frightening people away.[8]

Does Sex Sell?

A quick note on this topic, because "everyone knows sex sells." Or does it?

Based on recent research, the take away is that sex in advertising definitely gets people's attention. But not in the way marketers want. In a recent study, men remembered ads with sexual content, but less than 10% of them could remember the brand or product.[8]

This phenomenon was nicknamed The Vampire Effect, because the carnal content was sucking attention from the ad's real purpose.

In other words, yes, sex gets our attention, but its very, well, *distracting*.

Let's take an easy example: the word *titillate*. (Now, honestly, didn't you just giggle a little bit when you read that word?) If that's the emotional reaction you want your brand associated with, go for it. If not, don't.

Sidebar: A Lesson about Trust from Warren Buffet

Download any Berkshire Hathaway annual report and read Warren Buffet's letter to the shareholders. His tone is authentic, human…and trustworthy. He accepts full responsibility when his company makes bad investment choices. He talks openly about his mistakes with phrases like, "my actions have cost you money," and "I struck out." With multi-billions of dollars at stake, this level of honesty is one of the reasons Buffet is a financial super star.

Compare that to just about any other annual report letter — where the accepted approach is to avoid the bad news side of the truth by using excuses and verbal loopholes to spin things as positively as possible.

TRY THIS:

Ironically, the proof in the facts-versus-feelings debate can be defined by pure logic (those of you who studied logic in college will recognize the pattern).

- All human beings choose the option they feel most emotionally drawn toward. Therefore....

    - If your company does not create a positive emotional connection with your audience,

    - Then your audience will not choose you; they will choose the option that they DO feel emotionally drawn towards.

You can break through to new sales levels by developing trust through your content. Whether it's web copy, customer stories, or product demos, do your darndest to create content that doesn't seem like a sales tool. Rather than *pushing* information out, look for ways to *pull* your audience in — with relationship- and trust-building content.

Try creating your own trustworthy content

1. Get out of the habit of sell, sell, selling

Content that builds trust reads like an unbiased perspective, rather than a brand message pusher. Try setting a strategic goal that — whenever possible — you will create pieces that genuinely help your audience make the best purchase decision for themselves.

2. Be uncompromisingly honest

Being honest builds trust. When we create content, we need to tell the truth at all costs. Being relentlessly honest demonstrates integrity. Creating spin may be what we see others doing, but if you want to build trust, never give in to the temptation to modify or distort the facts.

One way to lose trust is to over-promise. In our haste to stand out from the competition, we don't want to risk having the customer feel that we've under-delivered. What about honestly stating what your strengths are... and what your strengths aren't?

3. Be unstintingly kind

Extending kindness is a mark of trustworthiness — and people trust people who are trustworthy. When people visit someone's house for the first time, they may bring a small gift to signify that they come in a spirit of friendship. This behavior encourages trust to develop. So, find new ways to create content that is genuinely valuable to your audience, like free knowledge or samples. Another way to be generous is to acknowledge the contributions of others within your company — and those in the wider market.

4. Be courageous in the face of bad news

I know of a woman who has a very successful online training brand and product. I recently Googled her product name, and the two listings at the top of the page had "scam" at the end of her product name. Turns out, some guy had started slamming her product on social media...and went on to create a website dedicated to discrediting her brand and product.

I don't know the backstory on this. But something happened that really upset this guy. Upset him enough to escalate his social media attacks into building a website dedicated to venting his anger. Whether his anger was justified or not, most people will respond to accusations like this with a "where there's smoke, there's fire" belief against you.

That's why it's essential to respond to "bad news" as quickly as possible, so you can turn the tide — and public opinion — to your favor.

If you ever started getting negative comments in your social media, it would be understandable to want to avoid the issue. It's very common to hope the negativity will go away on its own and be forgotten.

But what you need to do is the opposite: Face it and address it. ASAP. I see this as honorably standing tall in the face of conflict. That's what courageously honest people do. And human beings are deeply attracted to courageous honesty.

This can actually be an opportunity to stand out and build even more trust.

Don't make excuses or point fingers if you're in any way responsible. And definitely don't get into a "tit for tat," back-and-forth argument with the accuser. Instead, apologize, explain, and do everything you can to make things right — right away.

Handled well, you can demonstrate professionalism, objectivity, leadership, wisdom — even compassion — and garner more loyalty from your followers, and more trust from your prospective customers.

Try This in Social Media:
Depending on how you use it, Social Media can be a powerful tool for connection — or betrayal.

- **Listen.** In a trusted human relationship, the process begins with listening. Listen to your audience's hopes, fears, and problems. Listen to what's making them tick. Make sure your contributions show genuine interest in the problems of the people you are dealing with, *even if there is nothing in it for you.*

- **Be willing to learn.** No one likes (or trusts) someone who is always saying, "I'm here to tell you what you should know." Yes, of course you are expert in your field. But also demonstrate an openness — even a desire — to learn from your audience.

- **Create content that is NOT self-serving.** In a recent issue of Forbes, Toyota published an article about Toyota. The number of people who viewed it would fill about one quarter of a large sports stadium. But, in that same issue, Oracle published an article about innovation that didn't reference Oracle at all. That act of courage from Oracle attracted enough views to fill that sports stadium ... three times! [Data scoreboard: Toyota 14,000 views. Oracle: 300,000 views — and 55,000 shares.]

What's your Trust Rating?

Go to your website. Read the pages that talk about your company and what you offer. Now, based on what you've learned in this chapter, how much "real estate" has your company invested in building trust with your audience? Is there room for improvement?

Don't worry if you're disappointed in what you see, there's no need for a revolution. Evolution will do. Just start creating content that builds trust, step by step. Then measure the improved response — and see for yourself how powerful trust-building content can be.

CHAPTER 7

R – RELEVANT INFORMATION: IT'S YOUR SALES FUNNEL, BUT IT'S THEIR DECISION JOURNEY

> *"Learning is linking something you know to something you do not know."*
> — JIM KWIK, MEMORY AND LEARNING GURU

WE ALL LOVE a compelling conversation where the dialogue goes back and forth in a lively exchange. Don't you love how it feels to be in a conversation like that? Where both you and the other person are tossing ideas and perspectives back and forth, and you often say and hear things like, "That reminds me of something that happened to me...." Or, "That's like something I read the other day...."

That is how our brain works when it learns. When we receive new information, our brain first looks for any event in memory where we had a similar experience. It immediately looks for relevance. And then creates a mental simulation. Your brain's learning process always starts by creating a mental simulation of what's being described to you. If it can do that, you'll have a feeling of connection and engagement in the conversation. But if the idea is totally new, totally foreign to your experience, and there's nothing you can relate to about it, your mind will do the equivalent of spinning it's wheels, searching and searching for that connection — and you'll experience the sensation of confusion.

As the Jim Kwik quote above summarizes so well: association is the key. The only way humans learn is if we have a related experience under our belt that can be the seed for that new idea to grow from.

The accepted strategy for content creation is to shout out "ours is the best." But it doesn't matter how loud you shout it (with elaborate graphic design) or how long you shout it (with pages and pages of content). People learn and remember **only if** what they read or hear is related to a current or past situation in their lives. That's the only way their mind can create that emotional mental simulation. They need to be able to "see" it; they need to be able to "feel" it; they need to be able to "experience" it in their minds. If you help them do that, they are much more likely to re-examine the way they see things — which is the first essential step in persuasion. But they have to create a mental simulation that directly relates to their situation. That's the only way they can rethink it for themselves — and then rationalize "going in your direction."

Mental Simulation — the first step to persuasion

Mental simulation is the first step to persuasion. And persuasion is really about mindset transformation.

Your audience knows they need a way out of the bad situation they're mired in. But what they don't know is that they're also stuck in a *perception*. And your content needs to shift that perception; it needs to transform their mindset.

It's as though your audience has driven a car into the mud and gotten stuck. As the driver, they keep pressing harder on the accelerator. Sure, a lot's going on: the engine emits a deafening roar and mud is flying everywhere. But all that's happening is that the wheels are digging deeper into the mud. They're looking for a solution — they want to get back on the road again, but they're looking at it from the way they've always done it before: press on the gas and the car goes. Meanwhile, you've got a jeep with a winch, ready to pull them out, but they keep saying, "No thanks, I can do this myself." What's really important is to remember that the process that got them into the muck and mire is *Their Way* and people tend to defend *Their Way* and resist seeing things differently.

So what you need to do is understand THEIR situation and guide them in a process of "Mindset Transformation." You need to honor the situation they are in and the process THEY need to go through in order to change their mindset from seeing it their way to moving forward with your way.

It's your Sales Pipeline...but it's their Decision Journey

> *"Begin at the beginning and keep going until you reach the end."*
> — ALICE IN WONDERLAND

Virtually every business model presents the sales process as a Sales Pipeline or Funnel. We "pull" prospects into the pipeline, then we "push" them through to eventually become customers. But let's look at this from the audience's point of view, and see how that changes things: to them it's their Decision Journey. They don't care about your Sales Pipeline. They don't see themselves as a "prospect." They see themselves as being over-worked and under-appreciated ... with a major decision to make.

Now let's look at the Decision Journey from the perspective of mindset transformation.

To illustrate this, I'm going to use scenes from the movie *Star Wars* (otherwise now known as *Episode IV*). Even though there's always one person in every audience I've spoken to that hasn't seen it; I'm going to assume that person is not you. (If it is, then you're probably at least familiar enough with the story to be able to follow along…and if not, go check it out. It's a great movie. You won't be sorry.)

Star Wars creator, George Lucas, has always admitted that the story structure of *Star Wars* was far from unique. It was based on the same framework as all the great stories that come to us across time and cultures: *The Hero's Journey*. It's important to remember that in these stories, The Hero isn't always born with super-human abilities. Much of the time, The Hero is someone quite human, like Luke, who goes on a quest and is transformed by the adventure.

In fact, all of the great stories that come to us across time and cultures are about transformation. Either the Hero is transformed — or the Hero's world is transformed. There is no exception.

When it comes to mindset transformation, it's no exaggeration to say that your audience is in the same situation. They are living with a problem — and relying on a mindset that keeps them stuck there. But your content can transform their mindset so they are open to choose your solution…and when they do that, their life will be transformed for the better.

I use the cycle of The Hero's Journey to define the phases of The Decision Journey. That's because — in addition to being the framework for great stories (something we'll explore in more detail in Part III) — these motifs represent the process of mindset transformation.

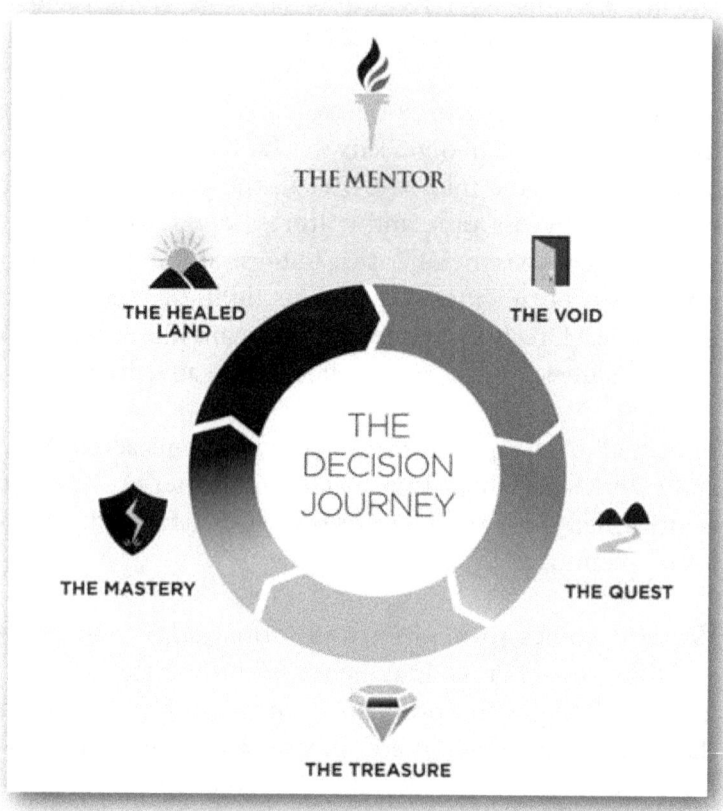

The Mentor

Remember the scene in *Star Wars* where *Obi Wan Kenobi* is training *Luke Skywalker* to become a Jedi Knight? Luke is "blindfolded" by wearing a blast helmet and is slashing at the air with his light saber, failing to hit the flitting *Jedi Training Ball* (yep, that's what it's called — I looked it up). Throughout the story, Luke relies on Obi Wan to be his source of wisdom as he moves forward in his quest to become a Jedi Knight.

For farm-boy Luke to become a Death-Star destroyer, Obi Wan Kenobi was indispensable in supporting Luke's transformation. That is the role of Mentor in every classic story: to give insight, training, and advice that helps The Hero move forward in his or her quest.

I can think of no greater focus for every piece of content we create: honest insight and advice.

We've already learned that feelings are more important than facts; that people do business with people they know, like, and trust. And, there's no better way to build trust than by offering helpful insight and advice throughout The Decision Journey.

That's the role of Mentor.

The HERO Method sees Mentor as The Guiding Light of your audience's experience throughout their Decision Journey. The goal is to create content that gives your audience the confidence to continue their Decision Journey *with you*, and to conclude that you're the right choice for them (if you really are).

Mentor is the foundation of ALL your content at every touch point in The Decision Journey. It is the source of the human and emotional connection that we've seen is essential.

Content that acts like a mentor supports readers in making essential mindset transformations: From doing it the way that's gotten them into the mess they're in, to doing it differently — with your product or service.

Phase 1: The Void

Something's missing in their world — and they may not even know it.

For the segment of your market that is in The Void, they're going through their life, stuck in a repeating loop that keeps presenting a problem. Some of them are not aware that the process they're using is broken. It may be inconvenient, but it's "just the way it is." They're simply going through their day the way they always have. If you had a video of their day, you could easily see that the way they're moving through their world is broken. But they don't see it that way. It's just the way it's always been done.

Or, maybe they're keenly aware that it's a problem, but solving it is not on the front burner, given all the other problems they have to solve. Even if they're aware that it's less than optimum, it's the devil they know. And they've figured out the "work arounds" that help them "get through the day just fine, thank you."

Regardless of the reasons for being mired in the situation, they're certainly not aware that their life could be better if your solution was in it. And, since these folks aren't looking for a solution, they're under the digital water line; they're not going to your web or social media sites.

How Mentor can be helpful at this stage

Since your audience is not actively looking for a solution, what works here is reaching out to them — with email and (yes) snail-mail, sales support tools (we'll talk more about these later), events (networking or otherwise), or advertising. What you'll use are specific Mentoring Messages that will help them see what's missing in their world because they don't have you in it. What you want to do is wake their minds up to the possibilities for change — help them see what their life could be like if they weren't mired in the mud of their situation.

Meaningful Mentoring Messages

1. To connect with audiences who are in The Void, the most important thing to do is to identify *what they can't do*; what they can't accomplish because you're not in their life.

a. Be very careful here. This is NOT telling them what you can do for them. It's very easy to fall back into "What we do is…." The scenario you want to paint for them is your understanding of what they're not able to do because they don't have you in their life. How are they limited? What's missing in their world? What can't they do? What can't they achieve without your help?

b. Paint a picture or pictures that they can relate to. Create those essential mental simulations. Create scenarios that they will immediately respond to with, "Yep that's the situation I'm in right now!" Just like the conversation we all like to be a part of, create content that they'll read and say, "That reminds me of something that happened to me the other day!"

c. Another reason this is important is that they may not be consciously aware that their process is broken. Think of the person in the car, stuck in the mud. There's no telling how long they've been there, pressing on the accelerator, doing what they've always done. Then, you walk up and gently tap on their window and point out the problem with something like, "Are you stuck in the mud, not getting where you need to go, no matter how hard you press on the accelerator?" That could be the "coffee" that wakes them up to the truth of their situation — which is the beginning of them seeing that there could be a better way....

2. How things can be easier.

   a. Now that you've gently painted an accurate picture in their minds about how broken things are for them, show them how their life could be so much easier if they had you in it.

For real-life examples and ideas of what you can create, go to <u>TheHeroMethod.com/TheBook</u>.

Phase 2: The Quest

The Quest begins when your audience says something like, "There's got to be a better way than how we're doing this!" "I wonder if someone else can help?"

Maybe the Quest begins because they received "The Void" Mentoring Message from you and it persuaded them to reconsider their mindset about "*The Devil They Know.*" But it can also happen for people who didn't get "the memo". Maybe they finally got fed up. Or, the problem had been on the back burner and it's now failed so badly they have to find a better way.

Another possibility is that *Word has Come Down from On High*) that this problem needs to be fixed…NOW. (Depending on your audience, the source of that Word can come down from various people in your audience's lives — anywhere from a boss to a spouse.)

This is when they're most likely to show up on your digital sites. That's why the content on your site must Mentor them through their Decision Journey from the very first moment they land on your home page.

Because, yes, The Quest is on, BUT there are forces that can cause them to never even add you to their short list.

The Rebel — "That's not how things are done around here."

Your audience could perceive you as The Rebel if they land on your site and think, "That's just not how things are done around here." Or, they may unconsciously feel resistance to the change you're suggesting they make because it's too radical. Either way, you won't have the chance to overcome their objections. They'll just anonymously bounce out of your site or unsubscribe from your email list, never to be heard from again.

How Mentor can be helpful at this stage

You can avoid being bounced off their "short list" of solution options by Mentoring your audience through any resistance.

Help them overcome the resistance to change. All human beings resist change. I've often heard the joke from sales people that to many prospects, The Perfect Solution is one that would fix the problem without changing anything. (I can relate to that. In 2005, I bought a Mini Cooper. I never bought another one because the new ones were different than the one I had. My ideal new car would have been exactly like the one I had...only new. But Mini never convinced me that I could *Motor* better in one of their new versions. So, I just kept driving the car I had.)

Mentor can help your audience overcome their resistance to change with relevant, mental-simulating content that calms their fears of change.

Meaningful Mentoring Messages:

1. Identify messages, stories, and design elements that show your audience (not tell them) what success can look like using your solution. Help them *envision* how successful they can be by doing it your way.

2. Show them (don't tell them) how easy it is to adopt your way. Help them see and feel how it can be easy (or easier?) to adopt your way of solving their problem.

These concepts may seem obvious. But your content must convey them in a way that paints those essential mental simulations. To transform your audience's mindset, you need to unconsciously stimulate the sensations of sight, sound, even texture. That's what I mean by show and not tell. You could say, "Erika was happy with the result." But can you feel the difference when you read, "When Erika heard the results, her face lit up and she jumped out of her chair, shouting, "Woo Hoo!" The first example is telling. The second example is showing. Of course, not every piece you create can use such storytelling techniques, but there's more room for it than you think. The fact is, something has to give. "State of the art" business communication only tells — and tells and tells (in it's attempt to sell, sell, and sell). Later on, in Part III, we'll dive into specific tips on how to create content that makes unconscious connections that show and not tell.

Another reason that showing is essential, is that our audience associates being told with being sold. And they emotionally perceive being sold as being manipulated — something their brains perceive as a threat. That's how traditional Features/Advantages/Benefits messaging *causes* bounce rates! Your audience's brains are emotionally withdrawing from the source of a perceived threat.

But if they experience a positive emotion to what they "see" and "hear" and "feel" — they'll be drawn towards you.

The Evil Empire

Another cause of getting bounced off the Short List is The Evil Empire — your competition. I call it The Evil

Empire in jest. Obviously, they're not Evil. But they can be an Empire. If your audience is going to your digital sites, they're going to the competition's too. And if the competition does a better job of reassuring your audience that their solution will make their life better, then you've lost another prospect to the competition.

How Mentor can be helpful at this stage
Fear not! There is a way to neutralize the effect of the Evil Empire's attempts to waylay your prospective customers.

How to Neutralize The Evil Empire:
It doesn't matter how big your competition is; how well-known their name is. Create relatable — or should I say "simulate-able" — content that connects with your audience on an authentic, emotional level. This will convince your audience to hang in there with you as they continue to move through their Decision Journey. The longer they do that, the more you can continue to connect with them.

And if you continue to do this better than your competition, prospects will choose you over even the biggest name in the business. (I've had clients choose me over bigger, more well-known consultants. They had a lot of pressure to choose them, but they chose me because, as one prospect-turned-customer told me, "I just feel more comfortable with you.")

The Quest summary: How Mentor can be helpful throughout The Quest

Using Mentor to overcome the causes of drop off, you can create content that convinces your audience to stay with you as they continue their Decision Journey.

Here are some of the roles The Mentor can play throughout The Quest:

Mentor can…

- Relate to their immediate needs…immediately

- Show them what success looks like — your way.

  - Help them "see" how successful they can be by doing it your way.

- Show them how easy it is to adopt your way

  - Help them "see" how it can be easy (easier?) to adopt your way.

For real-life examples and ideas of what you can create, go to <u>TheHeroMethod.com/TheBook</u>.

Phase 3: The Treasure

In sales and marketing, the "product as hero" point of view has been pervasive for years. But it is a broken assumption. One reason is because all your competitors are also telling your audience how great their "hero" is. Everyone's a "leader." Everyone's just won some kind of accolade. But what's on your audience's mind is: "I don't care about your awards; I don't care about your leadership in the market. I've been burned by businesses in those positions before. What I care about is the problem I have — and I need to know RIGHT NOW how your solution can help save me."

What we need to do is turn around 180-degrees. We need to see that The Hero is *our audience* who's on a quest for a solution to what's ailing their company or their life.

I know this is a mind-bending concept, but hear me out.

As we've seen so far, your audience is mired in a problem, and their perception about how things should be done has kept them stuck there. But now they're down to choosing the solution that they feel is best for them.

Whether your content is web content, a slide presentation, or product demo, the role of your content in this phase of their Decision Journey is to do more than help your audience **understand** your offer. Your content must inspire them to **want** your offer.

To do this we must transform their point of view — from seeing things "their current way" to seeing things "your new way." Only then will they move themselves forward in making a decision in your favor.

But thinking of your product as The Hero won't do this.

How The Decision Journey is like Star Wars....

The movie *Star Wars* begins with Luke Skywalker, living on a desert planet. Yes, it has a really cool binary sunset, but there's something missing in Luke's world — he's just not sure what it is. Then, The Empire kills his aunt and uncle, which impels Luke to join The Rebellion. This begins his Quest to master The Force. In doing so, Luke will end up making The Universe a better place.

This story is a metaphor for your audience's Decision Journey. Your audience (Luke Skywalker) is on a Quest to discover The Treasure (The Force) that will help make their life better.

That's why your solution isn't The Hero. Your audience is. Your solution is The Treasure they seek that will solve their problem. Being The Treasure is no small potatoes. They've got a big problem. And no one can solve it the way you can. But we need to shift our mindset to realize we are not The Hero — our solution is not The Hero — and it never has been.

I understand how this can feel radical. *But it can be a revelation.*

Accepted marketing "best practices" have taught us to be way too narcissistic about how we talk about our solutions. That's a huge reason why there's been an artificial cap on our potential response and revenue. What our audience has been hearing is us beating our chests in an attempt to tell them how great our solution is. If we're honest, we've been kind of annoying; maybe even being the guy who thinks the louder he is, the righter he is.

How Mentor can be helpful at this stage

You have every right to feel proud of the solutions you offer. You work very hard to make them the very best they can be.

But your audience doesn't really care about that. They don't care about the new or different *wiggledy gidget* you're offering. They care about their problems and their need to find a solution.

When we truly honor that this is Their Quest, that's when we'll be able to authentically connect with them — and that's when they will feel emotionally drawn to us.

And, if you continue to do that — while your competition continues to beat it's chest — your audience is much more likely to feel emotionally connected to you, and will therefore more likely choose your solution.

For real-life examples and ideas of what you can create, go to TheHeroMethod.com/TheBook.

Phase 4: The Mastery

This stage is where your audience is after they've chosen to buy your solution. Now that they have your solution, what they need to do is to "master" it. They need to get the most out of it.

Let's go back to the Star Wars metaphor.

Obi Wan Kenobi (as Mentor) introduces Luke to the concept of The Force (the Treasure). Then Luke, with Obi Wan's ever-present support, begins to master The Force.

How Mentor can be helpful at this stage

Usually in business communications, once the prospect buys the solution, the communications either end or are haphazard and sporadic. Too often, they're not relevant to their situation as customers. (Don't you hate it when you get emails that treat you like a prospect when in fact you're a customer?) But connection at this point in their Journey is as essential as ever.

When we communicate with customers, like Obi Wan's ever-present advice ("Use The Force, Luke."), we have the opportunity to develop deep loyalty that will cause the New Customer to recommend you to others and buy from you again and again.

Meaningful Mentoring Messages:

1. Thrill them with the experience of **becoming a customer.**

RELEVANT INFORMATION

- Make the on-boarding process as easy as possible.

  - Help them know what to expect. Do whatever you can to make the on-boarding process as thrilling as your solution. (The example that comes to mind is Apple's packaging. Clearly, they've thought the packaging through with as much care as any other aspect of their offerings.)

  - If your solution is a physical product, make sure it's easy to start using.

2. Thrill them with the experience of **being a customer**

   - Continually offer on-going training or advice on how to keep getting more and more from your solution.

   - Pay CLOSE attention to customer service communications.

You may think, "We've already got this down." But do you, really? Take an honest look at this phase. Is there any company you know that couldn't improve theirs? Maybe you could, too. You don't want one new customer to have Buyers Remorse. You want them to be delighted with the brilliant choice they've made.

3. Listen.

   - Whenever you receive a complaint, make sure that feedback doesn't land on deaf ears. Respond immediately with the heartfelt intent to resolve the issue at any cost.

   - Regularly send out surveys. Loyal customers will gladly give you advice about how to make Mastery Phase even better. Ask them how you could provide better customer service. Ask them what more they want to learn; what other solutions they might need. (This can give you creative ideas about possible new offerings that are pre-loaded with a market that needs them!)

I recently experienced *The Worst* on-boarding process. It was for a service that is designed to act as a mailbox for your snail-mail while you're traveling. You have your mail forwarded to them and they let you know via email whenever a mail piece arrives. You can ask them to shred it, open it and scan it so you can see what's inside the envelope — and all kinds of other nifty services. It's a great concept. But their onboarding process is horrific. When I reached out to them, without rancor, to tell them the problems I had, they were extremely defensive.

When I told another company (a common Wi-Fi provider on airlines), that their service was a No-Go and I wanted a refund, they didn't even bother to respond to my email. And took my Facebook comment off their site.

Not listening only makes the problem (customer dissatisfaction) worse. All the mailbox service had to do was respond with something like this — (IF this is true for them):

We're very sorry you have had so much trouble. We really appreciate your input and take it very seriously. Please believe that we are constantly working to improve our on-boarding process. Our goal is to make your experience with us nothing less than enjoyable.

As for the airline Wi-Fi service — all they had to do was give me a refund. It was only about eight bucks. By comparison, after using the mailbox service, I asked for a refund for something I was charged for, but didn't use. They didn't hesitate; they didn't ask for proof; they just gave me the refund. Even given the difficult on-boarding process, I would use them again. By giving me that refund, by trusting me, I have an overall positive emotional connection to their service. The positive emotional connection (of demonstrating their trust in me) overcame the negative experience (of the frustrating onboarding process).

IMPORTANT: Keep checking to see how well Mentor is doing

For each stage of the Decision Journey, there are different audience touchpoints. It's essential that you regularly check them **from your audience's perspective**.

This should be a regular process you go through. If you don't have the time to do it yourself, delegate it. Even if what you see "isn't pretty', you always want to know the truth of your audience's experience.

1. Imagine you're a customer — how easy is your website to navigate and find what you're looking for?

2. Create an "anonymous" email account and opt-in for an initial offer. This way, you'll see first-hand what your audience is experiencing. How well do your back-end technology systems work? Put yourself in the mindset of your audience — how effective is the content in moving you forward through your Decision Journey?

3. Go ahead and buy your own solution — then ask your support team the same onboarding questions a new customer would. How responsive are your customer service systems and people?

I recommend delegating these tasks to an outside virtual assistant — they'll give you a more accurate outside perspective than any insider can.

We need to never stop getting as much input as possible on this part of our business. It's too easy to not see the cracks in the foundation here, because we're looking in other directions — at all the other stuff on our plate. Meanwhile, the foundation of our customer experience could be seriously compromised and we would not know it.

Phase 5: The Healed Land

Again, back to Star Wars. Because Luke could use The Force to make that million-to-one shot, the Universe became a safer place.

Similarly, at this stage in the Decision Journey, because of your solution, your customer's world is a better place. The aspects that were missing in The Void phase are now whole, and because you've trained them so well in mastering your solution, they can do things they never even knew were possible.

They're delighted with their purchase choice, are able to make your solution dance, and their world is a better place because of it.

Now's the time to collect as many customer stories as possible and share those stories far and wide. (There's a lot more on how to create compelling customer stories in the next chapters.)

Please don't create customer stories with the purpose of sell, sell, selling. Create them with the intention of sharing stories about why others chose your solution; about how others are using your solution.

Collect Stories of Transformation that represent all of the phases of your audience's Decision Journey. Then share the stories that relate to the relevant stage the audience is in. (Share Void stories that offer helpful insight and advice for those in the Void phase; Quest stories that offer helpful insight and advice for those in the Quest phase, and so on.)

For real-life examples and ideas of what you can create, go to <u>TheHeroMethod.com/TheBook</u>.

How Mentor can be helpful at this stage

Keep the Mentor alive even now. When the time is right, you can honestly help customers see another Void that you can help them fill. You might have another solution that could be a perfect fit. Or there's another level of service that would be ideal for their situation.

And the cycle continues…

TRY THIS:

Instead of pulling and pushing your audience through YOUR sales pipeline, look at The Decision Journey as a holistic perspective of what your audience is experiencing. The way most businesses deal with prospects and customers, it's *sales* versus *marketing* versus *customer support*. But audiences don't care about the "departments" they're encountering. No matter where they are in their Decision Journey, the only thing audiences care about is how you can make their life better.

This model calls for breaking down the barriers between departments and extending truly customer-centric connections throughout all of your audience's Decision Journeys. This model also calls for a new leadership position within companies: A person with oversight to everything related to connecting with your audience. This person would ensure that at every touchpoint with your company, customers are receiving relevant, mental-simulating, mindset-shifting content at every phase of their Decision Journey.

1. Try NOT talking about how your product is The Hero that saves the day. (Remember: The Audience is the Hero. Your solution is The Treasure they seek.) By identifying with your audience as The Hero, they are more likely to identify with your solution — and *that's* more likely to shift their point of view. Try creating Mentor-oriented sales and marketing tools that are a source of honest insight and advice that will guide your audience in their quest for a solution.

2. Mentors train their protégés based on where their students are in the learning curve. See your audience as The Hero on a critical quest — and give them helpful insights that honor and support their mental process of transformation. Make sure your content authentically relates to your audience based on w*here they are in their Decision-Journey.*

    This pertains to your offers, too. Define offers that are relevant to your prospects wherever they are in their Decision Journey.

3. Stay awake to the human tendency to be self-focused …and right that wrong as quickly as you can.

Go to <u>TheHeroMethod.com/TheBook</u> for a pretty color version of The Decision Journey. It'll be a handy visual reminder and summary of how you can connect with your audience at each stage of The Decision Journey. No email address is required — just go to the site and download it.

PART III

HOW TO APPLY THIS NEW MINDSET IN CREATING CONNECTIONS

PART III

INTRODUCTION

O – Output: Using The Ancient Bones of Story in the Digital Age

> *"Not every experience makes a good story."*
> — ROGER C. SCHANK, DIRECTOR OF THE
> INSTITUTE FOR LEARNING SCIENCES

IT'S 100,000 YEARS ago and a one-armed elder sits around an open fire, those mysterious lights twinkling above in the fathomless dark. He is recounting an old story to the rest of his tribe. It's the tale of how his youthful lack of caution caused his near-death encounter with a lioness. The parents enjoy the story, even though they've heard it a hundred times. But the children's eyes are wide and unblinking. They are captivated. And they are learning.

That man most likely used the same building blocks of story that are found in all the great stories across time and culture. In my personal exploration of story, I have found these building blocks in international best-selling novels and in every world wide box-office-record-breaking movie. Some of these building blocks are story motifs, some of them are character archetypes. But they are all old. Very, very old. And we are hardwired to unconsciously resonate with them. That's why I call them The Ancient Bones of Story.

And it's The Ancient Bones of Story that we'll be exploring in this part of the book.

Given the buzz about story in the business world, why wait until this part of the book to start talking about it? When it comes to creating content, we've been like the driver in the car of the previous chapter. We've been taught to create content from various "Features/Advantages/Benefits" models. And if we're not happy with the results? We've been putting the model's "pedal to the metal." Hopefully, what is now clear is that creating content from that mindset creates bounce, not engagement and response — no matter how hard we press on the gas.

So now, our industry is buzzing about the need to create stories. It's become another item on our business communications check list. But why? As we've seen, a boring story will create bounce. An irritating story will create bounce.

INTRODUCTION

So clearly, creating story for the sake of story doesn't make sense. What does make sense is creating compelling content that is engaging and persuasive, and generates more response and revenue. And, yes, a well-crafted story contains all the tools we need to do that.

But what we're going to learn now is that we don't have to tell a complete story to achieve those goals.

The power of great stories doesn't come from telling them from the beginning to the end. Their power comes from being chock full of elements that connect with people on an unconscious level. The Ancient Bones of Story are where the power of story lies. These are the elements of story that click into and interact with our unconscious. They activate the parts of our brain that we've been talking about so far in this book. They stimulate emotion. They activate our sensory perception system (the place where those essential mental simulations are created). We are all hardwired to experience The Ancient Bones of Story in sensory terms in our minds — when we hear or read one of these Ancient Bones, we "see" it, we "hear" it, we can even "smell" and "taste" it. The Ancient Bones of Story also cater to the part of the brain that decides to trust; the part that says, "I'm open to change."

There could be no better frame of mind to cultivate in your audience. There is no other way to change people's mindsets. There is no other way to be truly persuasive. Research shows over and over again that when information is shared in the context of these Ancient Bones, the content is remembered more easily, accurately, and persuasively.[33, 36, 50, 53]

Just to reassure you: research has found these results in corporate communications. Mental simulations represent reality way better than numbers plotted on a bar chart. People who learned new concepts through The Ancient Bones of Story remembered that information more accurately and for far longer than new concepts that were relayed through facts and charts.[14, 33]

But to use these powerful elements, you must begin from a solid understanding of H (H2H connection) and E (Emotion not fact) and R (Relevant mindset shift) before you even begin to create your O (Output of content). Without that understanding, you'll lose the most powerful unconscious persuading forces of story. Put simply: If you don't have a good grip on H and E and R, your O is going to suck.

That's why I waited to talk about story until now. We had to first talk about what creates engagement and persuasion: how essential H2H connections are, how emotion not logic drives all buying behavior, and how relevance is the key to creating mindset shifts.

So now we're ready to dive into actually creating the output — the content for our websites, social media, and sales support tools (emails and slide presentations and such).

INTRODUCTION

This is where "unconscious content" comes into play. Unconscious content uses the Ancient Bones of Story to reach into our audience's unconscious mind and interact with them on that level — engaging them and persuading them that it's safe to do things differently.

What we're going to do in Part III is see how we can pull out any one of these Ancient Bones of Story and use them by themselves — or collectively — to create unconscious content that generates authentic and persuasive connections with our audience.

CHAPTER 8

MOTIFS OF TRANSFORMATION

The "spinal cord" of The Ancient Bones of Story is made up of the motifs and archetypes of transformation. Human, connecting content cannot live without them. We'll get to know them in this chapter and the next chapter. Then we'll learn how to use them.

These story motifs are the foundation of every classic book and movie across time and cultures. Human beings are hardwired to resonate with these Ancient Bones of Story. Use these ancient bones as the building blocks to create content with great bone structure (pun intended). Always keep in mind that your audience is hardwired to respond to these motifs.

The Ordinary World and What's Missing

The Ordinary World —
Every great story starts in The Ordinary World…and then the adventure begins.

> *Luke Skywalker's Ordinary World was the desert planet he lived on with his Aunt and Uncle.*

Think about The Ordinary World this way:
This is usually called "the target audience." But think about your audience in this more encompassing, more creative sense and you just might arrive at new demographics; new groups of people who you can help.

Think of The Ordinary World as the people whose world would be better if you were in it. Who are all the different kinds of folks who would care about what you have to offer?

What's Missing
The Ordinary World is always broken when a great story begins. But most of the time, no one knows it.

> *Luke Skywalker lives on a desert planet with really cool binary sunsets. But something's missing in his life — he just doesn't know what it is.*

MOTIFS OF TRANSFORMATION

Think about What's Missing this way:
How do things work in your audience's world BEFORE they have you in it? What are their most pressing issues because they don't have you in their life? What can't they do? What can't they accomplish? What can't the company achieve?

The Quest
The Quest is the reason for the hero's journey.

> *Luke's Quest is about mastering The Force. Harry Potter's Quest is about mastering witchcraft. Frodo Baggins' Quest is about destroying the One Ring.*

Notice how The Quest isn't about destroying The Evil One. Otherwise, Luke and Harry and Frodo would just be some other anonymous names in the crowd who are trying to defeat The Dark Forces. The Quest is always personal. The hero must always acquire special knowledge or skills in order to achieve the goal of the story.

Think about The Quest this way:
The Quest is about your audience (The Hero) acquiring the skills and knowledge they need in order to fix What's Missing in their Ordinary World.

The Call to Adventure

Every great hero is challenged to leave their Ordinary World in order to solve a greater problem. They may "Refuse the Call" a time or two, but to be a hero, they must eventually says yes to the adventure.

> *Even after Luke hears Leia say, "Help me Obi Wan, you're our only hope." He "Refuses the Call" of Obi Wan trying to convince him to join the rebellion. But when Luke returns home to find that The Empire has killed his Aunt and Uncle, his response is, basically: O.K., now I'm in!*

Think about The Call to Adventure this way:

This is the impetus that causes your audience to seek out a solution. They may be currently "refusing the call" by putting the issue on a back burner. But you know their world would be a lot better if they would put the issue on a "front burner" and say Yes to The Call.

The turning point in accepting The Call can happen when *Word Comes Down from On High*. The "Word" can come from a higher-up at work — or from a loved one in their life. Or, it could be an unexpected event (see: *Trickster* in the following chapter) that causes a "front burnering" crisis.

The Treasure

This can also be thought of as "The Elixir." It's what the hero needs to find in order to fix what's missing in

The Ordinary World. It's what will Heal The Wounded Land.

In Star Wars, The Treasure is the ability to master The Force — without going over to The Dark Side. Using The Force wisely is the only way to destroy The Empire.

Think about The Treasure this way:
The Treasure is the unique way your solution fixes What's Missing in your audience's Ordinary World. It's just the pure facts about what your solution is. No hyperbole, no "the best." Just the facts — *as they relate to What's Missing*. (It's what's in the Treasure Chest: 50 pieces of eight, 100 pounds of gold, 200 pounds of silver .... You get the idea.) Go through this process and you'll discover some very interesting things about your solution. You may discover that you have *not* been touting aspects of your solution that are actually really important. And, you may find that the *Wiggledy Gidget* you're highlighting on your home page isn't important at all to your website visitors. Defining the treasure is a great exercise in getting real about your solution. Which is essential for the next phase of the cycle.

The Mastery
This is when the heroes bring what they have learned during their adventure "back to the world" — and use it to Make the World a Better Place.

Luke returns from being trained by Obi Wan, and "Uses The Force" to destroy the Death Star. Harry uses the skills he has learned to destroy He Who Could Not be Named. And Frodo is finally able to destroy The One Ring by calling upon the inner strength he's gained from all his adventures.

Think about The Mastery this way:
The Mastery happens after your audience has purchased your solution. This is the process your audience needs to go through in order to master your solution. It does no good for your solution to "sit in a box on the shelf." What skills do they need to make your solution dance? What needs to happen for them or their company to get the most out of your solution?

The Wounded Land is Healed

All great stories end with a profound resolution. The Hero has said yes to The Call to Adventure — and has fully engaged in The Quest and The Mastery, learning the skills or insights they needed to master The Treasure. And because of that, The World (or the Hero's World) is a better place.

The Death Star, Lord Voldemort, and The One Ring have been destroyed — and every one of those worlds is a better place because of it.

Think about The Land is Healed this way:

Your audience embarked on a Quest, chose your solution, and learned how to make it dance. Their world is a better place because of it. Their world has been transformed compared to how things used to work in the Ordinary World. They now have what they really wanted. They now have what is most important to them.

CHAPTER 9

ARCHETYPES OF TRANSFORMATION

Now that we've explored the Ancient Bones of the *Motifs of Transformation*, let's get to know the *Archetypes of Transformation*. Exploring the *Motifs of Transformation* help us better understand our audience as they move through the *stages* of the Decision Journey. Exploring the *Archetypes of Transformation* help us understand the "*forces*" that are "behind the scenes" of the overall Story of Transformation.

The Hero

The Hero is not necessarily The Main Character of the story. What defines the Hero is that he or she is the one who is transformed by the adventure.

> *Luke is transformed from a farm boy to a Jedi Knight. I also see Han Solo as a hero. He is transformed from a heartless smuggler (who shoots first!) to a loving man and hero of the rebellion.*

Think about The Hero this way:
As we've discussed before, the Hero is your audience whose mindset is transformed by Their Quest for a solution to What's Missing in Their World. What makes the average person a Hero is their willingness to say Yes to the Adventure.

The Mentor
The Mentor is the source of wisdom that the hero taps into in order to discover and master The Treasure. The role of Mentors in all great stories is to give heroes helpful insight, training, or advice that moves them forward in their adventure. It is not possible for heroes to achieve their goal without The Mentor. Every great story has a source of wisdom that the hero learns from.

> *Obi Wan, Yoda, Gandalf — and many of the teachers at Hogwarts — were all Mentors.*

Think about The Mentor this way:
If the audience is The Hero, then The Mentor will give them the insight and advice they need to move forward in Their Quest, find The Treasure, and Master it. What is that source of helpful insight and advice for your audience? *It's every piece of communication you create.* Every touch point they encounter with your company in Their Quest must offer them helpful insight and advice on how to continue their Decision Journey; how to make the best decision for them or their company.

The Shadow
The Shadow is what keeps The Hero from finding The Treasure.

Darth Vader, Lord Voldemort, and The One Ring all wear the mask of The Shadow.

Think about The Shadow this way:
What keeps prospects from bringing your solution in? What keeps them from saying, "Yes"? These are usually fears, doubts, and confusion. Shadow can be thoughts and beliefs like: "I don't believe your offer can do what you're saying it can," "I'm confused about what your solution does," or "I doubt that your solution can help me."

Identify as many aspects of The Shadow as you can. By knowing The Shadow well, you as The Mentor can help The Hero overcome it. For example, let's say you know that people doubt your solution's ability to help them. You can create content that includes testimonials or customer stories that specifically illustrate how others overcame those same doubts or fears.

The Trickster
The Trickster is an unpredictable force that changes the situation. Just when the heroes think things work like so, The Trickster comes in…and everything changes. I happen to love Trickster. It is The Ultimate Change Maker.

It can be your best friend in getting your audience to start looking for a different way of doing things.

> *I'm going to switch examples here and move to "Pirates of the Caribbean". Remember when I said the hero is not always the Main Character? Captain Jack Sparrow is the main character. But he's not a hero. He's a Trickster. The heroes are the young lovers. They're the ones transformed by their adventures. Meanwhile, Jack Sparrow (excuse me: <u>Captain</u> Jack Sparrow) is never-changing. He is always unpredictable and loves nothing more than to shake things up. And in doing so, he is always causing the next stage in the adventure for the young lovers. He is a fabulous example of Trickster Personified!*

Think about The Trickster this way:

For your audience, Trickster is "the ground shifting underneath" them; things suddenly aren't working the way they have before — or something unexpected happens. (I'm remembering one of my mother's favorite sayings whenever life [Trickster] took her by surprise. She'd assert, "That's not supposed to happen!") Whatever it is that's "not supposed to happen" can be the very thing that motivates your audience to find a solution. Understanding the possible Trickster elements in your audience's life is a great way to connect with them. And it's a fabulous addition to any customer story and product demo scenario!

CHAPTER 10

METAPHORS

In 1939, physicists began talking about theoretical spatial anomalies called "Gravitationally Completely Collapsed Objects." They chose those words to describe what happens after suns die and collapse. To them, those words described the physics of it as simply as possible.

Back then, only a hand full of devotees were interested in "GCCOs." Then one fine day, John Wheeler coined the term "Black Hole." This was not an effort to "dumb it down." John Wheeler was no slouch in the world of physics. He was a colleague of Niels Bohr in exploring quantum physics, and worked with Albert Einstein on the unified field theory. And in renaming *Gravitationally Completely Collapsed Objects* to *Black Holes*, he changed the world. He instinctively turned this intellectual concept into a deeply symbolic — and compelling — metaphor.

At the time, this metaphor fascinated the world. People thought, "Wait a minute. There's something black in space…

but isn't space already black? And there's a hole in space? But isn't space already a vacuum?" What the metaphor could do that "GCCO" couldn't was create a mental simulation in people's minds that stimulated their curiosity — even though it was a completely foreign concept that most of them could never fully wrap their minds around. It wasn't just fiction writers who glommed onto the concept of Black Holes. Other scientists got interested ….the press became fascinated….and the research funds started to flow.

Today, Black Holes are a household name. There's no way Gravitationally Completely Collapsed Objects — or even GCCOs — could ever have achieved the same level of fame.

Does the GCCO naming process sound familiar? It should. We do this all the time in business. We create a new thing or a new idea, and in trying to explain it, we end up giving it a complex name. Aware that it's too complex, we try to simplify it by turning it into an acronym. The problem is that neither the name nor acronym can connect on the limbic level. They're too abstract. There's no connecting point where your audience can make a mental simulation.

That's what a metaphor can do.

Metaphors are a kind of shorthand that helps us quickly convey even the most complex concepts. Metaphors can describe the indescribable; explain what's unexplainable; by creating profound mental and sensory simulations.[47]

METAPHORS

If you're dealing with any new concept that's new to your audience, metaphor may be the only way to explain it to them. That's just how the brain works.

But don't use these powerhouses only to explain the complex. Use metaphors as often as you can to paint simulations in your audience's minds.

Here's an example: There is an *amazingly yummy* fruit called cherimoya. Having been born and raised in the United States, the first time I went to Peru was the first time I had tasted it. It's *the most delicious fruit I've ever eaten*. And when I tried to describe it to my friends back home, I immediately chose metaphors: The texture is creamy like pudding. And the taste is of sweet vanilla with a hint of plum. (Is your mouth watering?)

Notice the difference: What was your reaction when you read my description of "amazingly yummy" and "the most delicious fruit I've ever eaten"? Even having used italics to emphasize the words, I'll bet money your reaction was emotionally neutral. You didn't have any interest in it; you weren't intrigued. But what about when you read that it's like vanilla pudding with a hint of plum? Again, I'll bet money that *that's* when you became intrigued. That's when you thought…." Ooh, I'd like to try that." That's the difference your content can make. When you're using hyperbole to describe your solution as The Best, you're missing the mark. Use metaphor whenever you can, and you'll be bringing this powerful connecting effect to your content.

Here's another example: "Iron Man" is not a technically accurate name for this Super Hero. His suit isn't made of iron; it's a gold-titanium alloy. But "Gold-Titanium Alloy Man" just doesn't have the same ring to it. Iron instantly symbolizes solidness, strength and durability; toughness. But the phrase, "Gold-Titanium Alloy" just sits in the neo-cortex, spinning in cognitive space without making any deep, limbic connection.

Symbols — Visual Metaphors

Symbols have been part of human culture since the beginning of human culture.

Symbols are, of course, ubiquitous in religions. But they're also all over the business world. Apple owns 300 icons; Microsoft owns 500. And then there's McDonald's Golden Arches and Nike's "swoosh."

If you don't think symbols are powerful, I have one word for you: Swastika. I'll bet money your brain just lit up with emotion, whether you're aware of it or not. I found it fascinating when I discovered that the swastika has been a sacred and auspicious symbol in Hinduism and Buddhism. The oldest version found goes back 10,000 years. But to people in "the west," it is associated with the horrific power of Nazi fascism.

Humans use symbols instinctively and respond to them unconsciously. In 2009, Iranian demonstrators waved green

METAPHORS

flags in the streets as a symbol of their cause. And, during the Orange Revolution in Ukraine in 2004, women and senior citizens stood at the front of the protesting crowds handing flowers to the military.

Do symbols work in business communication? Of course they do. We're all hardwired to respond to them. A well-placed symbol will create deeper connections with your audience than words alone. One of my clients focuses on finding ways that clients spend money unnecessarily. In a way, they're finding "hidden money." My designer found the perfect visual symbol to represent this: a businessman using a shovel to dig down toward a huge dollar sign. When visitors go to the site, that visual stands out. Even if they never read a word on the home page, that symbol will stay with them.

According to a recent study, press releases that included visual elements increased the visibility of a press release by nearly 10 times. I would add that the more symbolic that visual is, the higher the response will be.[24]

The best example I can think of that you are likely to be familiar with — in terms of using visual symbols to persuade — is the "*1984*" Apple Ad. I'm sure you remember it: it features a powerful athlete, running with a huge mallet. She runs into a hall filled with people who are all dressed alike in blue. They seem to be in a trance, watching a projection of a disembodied head speak to them about "the glory of information purification." She "discus throws" her mallet at the projection screen — and blows it up.

In my book, this ad is pure genius. There are symbols and metaphors in there that I didn't even understand when I saw it (the "blue" audience represented "Big Blue" — IBM, The Evil Empire at the time). Even though I didn't understand that, the ad was so rife with universal symbols, I found it — as did millions of others — to be mesmerizing. And highly memorable.

It was powerful in another way; it was so successful as a Super Bowl ad that it began the frenzy of creating multi-million-dollar Super Bowl ads. But as it often happens, companies try to duplicate success, but they miss what the real driver of that success was. As in this case, it's never the amount of money spent. It's the message that made it powerful — and the message was conveyed by symbols.

Words as metaphors

Remember the chocolate-versus-carrot cake scenario we discussed earlier? When you perceive a cake as "chocolate," your brain "draws you toward it." But when you learn that it's carrot cake, your brain sends out chemicals that draw you away from it. That's the power of words. Every single time we see a word we feel positive about, our brains draw us toward it. Whenever a word strikes us as unpleasant, our brains move us away from it.

In a similar way, when you read the phrase, "having a rough day," the word "rough" causes sensory areas of your brain to be activated. But when you read the phrase, "having a bad day," no sensory areas are activated.

METAPHORS

When research subjects read phrases that described actions like "biting a peach" and "grasping a pen," specific areas of their brains lit up. Later, when the same subjects watched videos of other people doing these same things, their brains lit up in the exact same regions.

Try it yourself: Read the words "nails scratching a chalkboard." Did you just cringe? Now read the words, "sucking on a lemon." Do you notice your salivary glands kicking in? What about "cockroach scuttling up your leg." Did you just say, "*Ew*!"? Your mind, whether you're conscious of it or not, is simulating that irritating sound, the sour taste, and those insect legs crawling over your skin. What's happened is that your brain has lit up exactly as if it were happening to you. This is how the words we read and hear affect us long before our conscious minds are aware of them.[8, 50]

A TV commercial showing a person savoring the aroma of freshly brewed coffee can trigger these same olfactory sensations in viewers. In fact, just reading this has done the same in your brain. The areas of the brain that light up when we see — or read about — an activity are identical to those that light up when we actually experience it.

Why is this important? Because words that simulate sensations are powerful in business communication. A recent study even connected sensory adjectives to higher sales!

Be aware of every word you use. Every word is important. Let's compare *expert* versus *partner*. For one of my clients,

I used "experts" to describe my client on their home page, but used "partners" in their customer stories. That's because when prospects are first coming out of The Void phase (and landing on the website for the first time), they're looking for assistance. They for sure want expertise, but not necessarily a partner. Yes, they're looking for a date, but not to get married. Then, when customers are further into The Quest (and interested in customer stories) they will read about other happy customers who see my client as a long-term, trusted partner. This simulates the emotion in readers of having a committed, trusting partnership — an emotionally positive association that I want them to have about my client.

CHAPTER 11

CREATING THE OUTPUT — WEBSITES

When most visitors come to your website, it's because they are in The Quest phase of their Decision Journey. They're not needing a flashy interactive experience ... what they're needing is help in making a decision. Recent research indicates that the most common variable associated with website stickiness is "decision simplicity" — how easy it is for visitors to gather trustworthy information that helps them weigh their buying options.[54]

Again, this sounds like a no-brainer. But how many of us are actually strategizing our websites to do this? In the marketing world, building a website begins with a process called "messaging." "Messaging" in this sense is a list of things we want to tell our audience. Typically, messaging ends up being based on that old "Features/Advantages/Benefits model — and are way too self-referential to be of much use.

What I'm proposing is that we develop messaging that *identifies with our audience's situation* — and defines the helpful insight and advice our audiences need to make a good decision for themselves.

In other words, don't start with you and your awards. Start with how you can help. If you'll remember, this is the role of Mentor — to always offer helpful insight and advice throughout the Decision Journey.

Instead of identifying your key Features, Advantages, and Benefits, ask yourself these questions: How can our content do a better job of helping people know, like, and trust us? How can we give them better insight and advice about making the right decision for their situation? How can our content create mental simulations of our solution that persuade them to put us on their short list, to keep us on their short list — and to choose us as the best solution (if it authentically is the best solution for them).

Let me be clear on that last point: I believe that if a visitor comes to your site and your solution is not a good fit for them, you should not try to sell it to them. Even if it just involves them asking for, negotiating, and getting a refund, that's an operational expense you don't need to go through. On the other hand, if it's a more complex solution and it's not a good fit for them, they could end up being a very expensive client — always needing hand holding, or special attention. So, yes, you may make a one-time sale, but it could end up costing you more than what you've made.

But, if you honestly let them know that another solution would be a better fit for them, they are that much more likely to trust your insights and advice — which means they'll come back when the time is right and you are both a better fit. Either way, they are much more likely to recommend you to people who are a good fit.

But if you try to fit their square peg into your round hole, they're not going to be happy…and that's not going to be a win for anyone in the long run. Again, this warrants a discussion about the role of overall Customer Connection throughout The Decision Journey — rather than the show being driven by sales quotas. (I'm not saying I have the answer; I know this is a tough nut to crack; I'm just saying it warrants a discussion….)

Tips for creating websites that connect:

I have analyzed over 100 websites. And here are some patterns I continue to see that cause bounce — and can be easily fixed. These are concepts that people often say, "Oh, we've got that covered." I believe these companies truly think they are connecting with their audience.

But when I go to their site, I quickly see that they're not. Like the driver in the car that was stuck in the mud in that previous chapter, it's easy to assume that since our *intention* is to connect with our audience, that's what our content is doing. But what my analysis shows time and again is that most companies talk AT their visitors with self-focused content instead of giving their audience relevant information in a compelling way that makes it easy to choose the solution that's right for them.

1. How do you solve their most pressing issues?

Everyone who reads your content has a challenge. They're also overworked and don't have time to figure out how you can help them. Telling them what you do does not help them see how you can help them. It's important to tell your audience right away how you help them overcome key obstacles in their lives in ways no one else can. Here's an idea for you about that:

"Above the fold" refers to the part of the web page visitors see first. They scroll down to see the rest of the page. This is the most valuable "real estate" on your website. That's because it's the moment when people will either stay and visit some more — or decide there's somewhere else they'd rather be.

Most companies use this area to highlight benefits to their customers or awards they have won. The problem is, your audience is probably reading similar messages on your competition's websites. My question is: Do your key messages clearly differentiate your company — *in terms of how you can help visitors achieve the results they're yearning for?*

To get to these core messages, refer back to Chapter 8 and figure out what's missing — what's broken — in their

Ordinary World because you're not in it. Then define how you specifically "heal what's broken" and make your audience's world a better place. I often create a simple before/after table, listing What's Broken (What's Missing) on the left, and what things will look like after their Land is Healed on the right. Messages of transformation like this will show your audience how their world can be transformed. These are essential mental simulations that are absolutely necessary for any kind of mind shift, any kind of persuasion, to take place.

It's also a great way to differentiate your company from the competition, because I'll bet money they're not reaching out to your audience with stories of transformation like this.

2. Create an emotional connection.

As we've learned, emotional connections open people up to the rationale you want to get across. Every buy — even the most technological buy — is an emotional buy. It may take a bit of courage — maybe even a lot of courage — to weave emotion into your home page. But you need to make that emotional connection of trust right away! The longer it takes for visitors to get a positive emotional read about you, the higher the chance they'll bounce out, never to be seen again.

Why? Because that's how humans evaluate relationships. Think about it: When visitors come to your home, you do your best to make them feel welcome. You greet them at the door, guide them to a comfortable seat, offer them something to drink. *Then*, if you have some great news about yourself you want to share, you talk about that later.

I recommend you do the same with your website visitors. One way to do this links back to recommendation #1: use some of the valuable "real estate" on your home page — the place where people are first connecting with you — to talk about how you help them overcome their challenges in ways no one else does. Then use that copy to link them to the rich information you have that relates to those differentiators.

Immediately create a personal connection with your audience. Do that, and they'll be more likely to *like and trust* you. That means they'll visit more pages, remember more information, take more positive steps toward a sale, and have positive associations with your company and your brand.

3. Give them something of genuine value.

A big part of *knowing*, *liking*, and *trusting* is in the *receiving*. Being generous tells your audience that you see your customers as long-term partners, not as a series of one-time sales. I believe it's important to leave people feeling that visiting your site (or reading your collateral, or watching your presentation) was of genuine value to them; that it was truly helpful in some way.

Why is this important? Like everything else in this book, there's an important neurological model backing up this strategy. We talked about reciprocity in an earlier chapter.

It's when human beings receive something free, their brains are wired with the "need" to reciprocate. Give your visitors helpful insight and advice for free — and they will be neurologically "driven" to return the favor. One of the interesting things about reciprocity is that when a human being receives something, they often give back something of far greater value than what they initially received.

So, try offering your website visitors a Free Gift with no strings attached. For example, give them a truly valuable e-book — without asking for their email address. In their minds, the reciprocity loop won't be closed until they have given something back to you. Somewhere in the Free Gift, offer something else of even more value, with a link that now asks for their email address. This strategy will stand out from the crowd because most companies start out by asking prospects for their very valuable email address. But you started out with a truly Free Gift, and THEN asked to deepen the relationship by asking them to entrust you with their email address. After that, as you continue to connect and be generous, they're more likely to reciprocate by choosing you.

[Side note: this is not a list-building strategy. This is a relationship-building strategy. If you need to build your customer list, then asking for their email address in order to receive your "Free Gift" is OK...*but*... See more on this in the next section.]

On the other hand, if you don't give them something of value, you risk making visitors feel like they're being sold to. When that happens, their defenses go up. Sure, they may gather some information, but no relationship of trust has begun.

So, make sure your visitors leave your site feeling it was helpful to them. They're more likely to remember what they've read, and more likely to like and trust you.

More on pre-qualifying for "free" offers

As you can tell, I'm not universally sold on asking visitors for their contact information in order to receive free stuff. Why not? Well, a few reasons. First, in terms of reciprocity, you're asking your audience to give you something (their valuable contact information) BEFORE you've given them anything. That's just not how humans work. It means your "free" offer is not perceived as free. And, if they perceive their contact information to be more valuable then your freebie, they're not going to sign up. It may also feel like you're "moving too fast" — asking them to marry you before you've gone on a date. Third, we are all already inundated with too many emails. And the last thing we want is to be on another company's e-sales list.

If you want to capture emails, here are a few ideas.

- Create a video that offers something of true value — and place it on the same page as your email-asking Free Gift. (Maybe have it be an auto-start video that starts playing the minute they land on your site.) In this scenario, the video is giving them something of value, then you're giving them the option to reciprocate by giving you their email address in order to receive an even more valuable Free Gift. As part of the opt-in process, be sure to reassure people that everything you send them will always be of value to them, and you've covered all the bases of resistance!

- Offer something especially cool that they understand involves sharing their email address as part of the deal. For example, the really cool thing could be a *truly* informative and intriguing webinar that they sign up for. That way, asking for their email address isn't an obvious attempt to capture their email address. Giving you their email address makes sense to them...and is of value to them. You'll use it to send them related links in order to attend. (Best case scenario, you'll also use it to send them more freebies before the webinar to build trust and interest — which will increase the likelihood that they'll attend.) In this scenario, it also makes sense to gather qualifying information, like their title and company size, because that will help you customize the webinar to make sure everyone gets the most out of it. As part of the opt-in process, be sure to let them know that's why you're asking for the extra information. But don't ask too many questions (the more questions, the more bounce.)

- Give your audience something *with no strings attached*. It's a great way to support your brand. And, if you create materials that are truly helpful, they'll want more. So, all you need to do is add *a prominent "call to action" in the information piece itself* — in an *H2H* tone — that invites them to receive more helpful information from you on a regular basis. In other words, you're still inviting them to sign up for your mailing list, but AFTER you've given them something for free.

Remember: Once you get their email address, don't mix in sales messages with your free tips sequence or you will erode the trust you're hoping to build. You can send occasional separate "sales" emails as part of a different email sequence — as long as the frequency of the free valuable information easily outweighs the number of sales emails.

A Word about Visuals and Video

There's a good reason to include lots of visuals and video on your website: We are not genetically designed to read (that's not easy for me to say as a copywriter who sweats over every word — but it's true). When we read, our brains are deciphering all the letters individually as symbols for sounds that then come together into words. Yes, it happens fast, and our brains learn to read based on context, but it's a lot of cerebral work.

We are, however, genetically designed to look at visual elements and watch video. Eye-tracking research shows that on any given page, the human eye jumps first to a human face, then to any design element, then last to copy. The most highly-read copy on any page is caption copy that's underneath a visual.

So here's an easy one: include photos of smiling faces. Humans can recognize a smile in microseconds — faster than we recognize any other facial expression. And, seeing a smile simulates smiling in our brains — releasing positive, feel-good chemicals, creating instant primal connection.

In the Metaphors chapter, we explored the power of visual symbols, which I highly recommend using in websites. Look for symbols that support your message and use them!

I also highly recommend creating videos. Valuable videos can be done inexpensively; they don't have to look super polished. I've seen very persuasive videos done with a smartphone!

However — like story — not just any video will do. Please don't create the typical "talking head" videos where you or your customers are telling the audience what a great solution you have. Everyone knows they're thinly disguised advertisements — which translates to: very expensive causes of bounce. But when they're done right, the content of a video can reach into the limbic brain and create deep connections. That's why I help clients build videos based on The Ancient Bones of Story.

For examples of videos based on The Ancient Bones of Story, go to TheHeroMethod.com/TheBook.

TRY THIS:

Use the trust-building influence of Mentor's insight and advice. It will be a powerful force in convincing your audience to stay with you as they continue their Decision Journey. Here are some things you could try — some of them may sound familiar — I've recapped them from the "Relevant" chapter about how Mentor's role can apply on your website:

- **Relate to your visitors' immediate needs…immediately.** For some clients, I've gone so far as to pose the question right up front on the home page: *What's your most pressing need?* And let visitors enter the site based on the 3 or 4 most pressing issues they're facing.

- **Show them what success looks like — your way.** Help your audience "see" how successful they can be by doing it your way. Identify messages, stories, and design elements that show them (not tell them) what success can look like using your solution. Help them create mental simulations of how successful they can be by doing it your way.

- **Show them how easy it is to adopt your way.** Help them "see" how easy — or at least easier — it can be to adopt your way of solving their problem. This is essential for helping them overcome their resistance to change.

- **Connect with your audience on an authentic, human level.** If you do this better than your competition, chances are good that more prospects will choose you over even the biggest name in the business.

- **Give stuff away for free.** Being generous is a great way to stand out from the competition. Build meaningful relationships over time by continually sharing valuable information with your audience, rather than always trying to sell them something. What about creating an *information-rich* autoresponder sequence; a series of connections that helps them overcome their key challenges?

- **Create valuable resources.** Lots of large organizations' websites have a "Resource" tab on the main navigation bar. Do what they do, only better. Website visitors have come to expect that "Resource" is just an extension of The Sales Department. Most "Resource Libraries" are filled with content that's based on what the company wants visitors to know about their company or solution. Don't make that mistake. Try surprising visitors with a resource center that has valuable information in the form of special reports, e-books, tools, or videos. Create content for your Resource Library by thinking in terms of what your audience would perceive as truly helpful in making their decision about the Treasure they're seeking.

CHAPTER 12

CREATING THE OUTPUT — SALES SUPPORT TOOLS

In this chapter, we'll dive into how to use The HERO Method to create the most common Sales Support Tools — emails, slide presentations, webinars, customer stories, and giveaways.

Email

> *Dear Reader:*
> *On a beautiful late spring afternoon, twenty-five years ago, two young men graduated from the same college…*

So begins perhaps the most famous letter in marketing history. It is certainly the most lucrative. This two-page letter was created for The Wall Street Journal, was in continuous use for 28 years — and generated an estimated one billion dollars in revenue. You read that right: One billion! I've analyzed the letter and what is clear to me is that the letter is a shining example of the power of creating relevant mental simulations. It begins by creating a mental simulation of the graduation, and even when it moves into a friendly sales speech, the mental simulations continue. (If you want to read the whole letter as it arrived in my mailbox, go to TheHeroMethod.com/TheBook.) The letter ends by turning the narrative into a story of transformation — suggesting that one of those men became a success (while the other didn't) because of the information he gleaned from The Wall Street Journal. Yes, it was a snail-mail letter, but the reasons it generated all that revenue work the same today as they have throughout human history. Because it connected with human beings in the way human brains are designed to respond.

I've heard it said that the in-box is nothing but an organizing system for other people's agendas. But what if our content could create mental simulations that our audience relates to? If we could do that, writing to them in a human, conversational tone about issues that are important to them, they will read it. And they will respond.

I wrote an email like that for one client — and the response was so high it crashed the server.

This again is the role of Mentor — to shift from making sales pitches to becoming a trusted partner. Aspire to use email as a way to become a reliable collaborator, and your audience will look to you for advice and dialogue about issues that concern you both.

Slide Presentations and Webinars

Oh, yes. The dreaded PowerPoint. Every one of us hates slide presentations with slides filled to brimming with words that the presenter just reads off the slide. And complex charts and graphs that confuse rather than clarify.

It's amazing to me how even storytelling webinars are painfully boring and confusing.

There are lots of great books out there on how to create the un-typical slide presentation. And, here's what The Hero Method has to add to the discussion:

- Be a human being who wants nothing more than to create authentic connections with your audience around the subject you're presenting.

- Find the most powerful symbols, photographs, or other images you can that visually represent the facts you want to relay. Then, reduce the words on your slides to absolute minimums and freely use those visual symbols. You can use the visual symbols to remind you of what you want to be talking about at that point in the presentation. Then, while the visual is up on the screen, share your expertise on the topic in a way that stimulates mental-simulations in your audience's mind. In other words: Use metaphors; tell stories that support the concept; use words that generate sensory reactions.

- If you have to use charts and graphs, make them VERY simple. Make them so easy to grasp that it only takes a few seconds to fully understand their meaning. (Think: Al Gore's "hockey stick" graph related to global warming.)

- Most important: Be Human. Bring your authentic enthusiasm for the subject. Authentic enthusiasm is contagious — and persuasive!

Customer Stories

You can think of a customer story as a long testimonial about a customer's experience with your company. Customer stories can be intriguing and compelling content that overcomes even the most powerful Shadow (resistance to saying Yes to your Treasure). Or they can be boring and irrelevant and a waste of your audience's time.

Recently, I was brought in to one of the biggest technology companies in the world to revamp the way they told customer stories. There was a genuine desire to create more compelling stories, but they were so mired in the mud of how they'd always done it, they weren't able to fully take their foot off the proverbial accelerator. In the end, the stories of transformation were still there. But after all the rounds of edits, with various people offering their feedback (based on The Old Way), the human interest got waylaid, and all the emotion got stripped out. The stories ended up reading much the way they always had — dispassionate, objective commentaries that connected with the logical, cortical mind of the reader instead of the emotional, limbic brain — which is the only place where connection and persuasion take place.

This is a morality tale about how difficult it can be, even with the best of intentions, to shift to a new way of doing things.

But it's also good news for smaller, more versatile companies about how you can outmaneuver The Big Guys. Smaller businesses are not so entrenched in The Old Way; there are fewer people involved who are resistant to change, which means it's easier for you to shift your marketing mindset and create truly compelling content. Meanwhile, I can assure you, The Big Guys are still stuck in The Old Way. And, because people do business with people they feel connected to, when your audience reads your compelling stories, they're more likely to choose you than The Big Guys.

Pull out the storytelling stops...

Customer Stories are the perfect opportunity to pull out all the Ancient Bones of Story into a complete, engaging narrative. But they need to be approached with care, as the morality tale above proves.

Instead of creating "case studies" based on the typical analytical outline of The Challenge, The Solution, The Benefits, I look at customer stories as "stories of transformation." How did the company or person go from their "Ordinary World" — where something important was missing — to the "Healed Land," where now their world is a better place because you now exist in it.

Let your customer stories show how you and your customer used your combined knowledge and experience to make the Main Characters' lives better — and the customer's world a better place. (Not: how did you come in and save the day.)

Be sure to include any unexpected events (Trickster) that happened along the way. Overcoming unforeseen obstacles is a storytelling crowd pleaser. They also make the story feel more true to the audience — because everyone knows nothing ever goes as planned.

How to "HERO-ize" your customer stories:

H — Human-to-Human (H2H)

The story must have human interest. That means there is a Main Character (or 2 – but no more than 3) at the center of the story who readers (or viewers, if it's a video story) can relate to. If the story is about a company, the story isn't about the customer — it's about the people and how they were involved in — or experienced — their company's transformation. In other words, the transformation of the company will be shown through the eyes of the Main Characters.

If the story is about an individual, then the story is about that individual's story of transformation as seen through their eyes....and, if pertinent, the eyes of those around them.

For example, one of my clients' stories began in *The Ordinary World* with their CFO struggling to make good decisions for the company. Her "world was broken" because she was inundated with paper reports that were confusing, contradictory — and mostly useless. But it was the devil she knew, so she soldiered on. Then, *The Trickster* suddenly appeared and changed everything when their business automation vendor told her they would no longer be able to respond to her needs. Thus, began *The Quest* — her company had to start searching for a better solution. They were about to go with another vendor when they were introduced to my client at the 11th hour. They chose *The Treasure* (my client). Now her *Land is Healed* because she has a quick and easy way to make fully informed decisions for her company. And, her company's world is a better place, because it has enjoyed steady growth ever since.

That's of course, the summary of a longer story, but you get the gist. It's not about "The Challenge" for the company, it's about what was missing for a human being. It's not about "The Solution," it's about how she's able to get what she needs to do a better job. It's not about "The Benefits" to the company; it's about how her life is better and how the company has been transformed.

Can you see how much more relatable that is? Even if you have a different job, you can relate to this person and her frustrations — and what it would feel like to work with a trusted partner to "right the wrongs" of the company's current technology. And it's easy to imagine how great it would feel to do your job so much better — and to be a part of helping your company succeed.

E — Emotional Resonance

For customer stories that stand out, you must connect emotionally with your audience. As we've seen, mental simulations create that much-needed emotional response. How do you tell your story in a way that's emotionally meaningful to your audience? By repeatedly asking yourself these questions:

- What was missing in the Main Characters' world. What couldn't they do because we weren't in their life?

- How did we help make the Main Character's life better?

- What unexpected events happened that we helped overcome that would give the story more reader interest? (Look hard for these, they're hugely helpful to include — they add interest and truth to the story.) The best ones are "Trickster" events that you worked together to overcome.

- From the Main Character's point of view, how was the company transformed?

Create the story using a fresh voice: Accept my "no jargon" challenge — write in an authentic, conversational tone — and see what magic emerges.

R — Relevance

Every customer has a number of possible stories you can tell. Find the best one by thinking first about your audience (as always). When you understand "What's Missing" in their world because you're not in it yet, you can clue into what kind of story of transformation will be the most inspiring to them.

Customer stories have unique power in Mentoring audiences, because they are an opportunity to really reach in and connect with them on a deep, limbic level. It's a unique opportunity to create those essential mental simulations because now you can pull out the stops in using metaphors, evocative words, and emotion.

Choose a story to tell that has these essential components:

- The events that take place are the most relevant — and meaningful — to your audience based on the role they play in their work or their life — and where they are in Their Decision Journey.

- The events come together to tell a powerful — maybe even inspiring — story of transformation. It moves from "What's Missing in The Ordinary World" to "The Land is Healed," using whatever motifs and archetypes are part of their story of transformation.

- The story comes together Mentor-like, offering real-life insight and advice that helps your audience move through their Decision Journey.

O — Valuable Output

The goal of every communication piece you create should be to play out the role of Mentor. To be a source of helpful insight and advice.

As is true for all the other content you create, get the H and the E and the R under your belt first. Then it'll be much easier to create a story that is relatable and inspiring — a story that's perceived as valuable, not as a manipulative sales tool.

e-Books

A well-known social networking service recently produced an e-book about demand generation. This "e-book" had all the look and feel of a brochure, and none of the value of a book. Unfortunately, "e-books" that are obviously trying to sell us something have become common in our world. Please don't follow their example.

Instead, look at e-books as a great opportunity to connect with your audience and build trust by giving them something of genuine value. This is an opportunity not to be wasted. If the content is about selling them, you've lost the chance to build a deeper, more trusting connection.

In creating an e-book, follow the same guidelines as Customer Stories. Yes, you're sharing information. But if you "HERO-ize" it, you'll create a page-turning e-book that's far more persuasive than anything your competition is putting out.

Story of transformation — Begin your e-book in the reader's "Ordinary World." Talk about how things work for them now, or how they perceive things now — and how something's missing, something's broken about that. Then take them through whatever Motifs of Transformation make sense to support your "story." Be sure to give your e-book a happy ending by taking them to the "Healed Land," where they can "see" how their world can be a better place because of the new information or perspective you've shared with them.

Human-to-Human (H2H) — The book must have human interest. If there's no real person involved in what you're sharing, then include examples of what you're talking about in the form of scenarios or mini-stories that involve humans. Those humans can come from many places — a well-known figure from the past, a customer (either real or fictional), someone in a different market altogether, or an employee at your company.

Emotional Resonance — As with every other piece of communication you create, connect emotionally with your audience. The "no jargon" challenge applies even more here than anywhere else, because with more length comes more possibilities to slide back into old habits.

Relevance — What information will be the most intriguing or inspiring to your readers? E-books can be powerful Mentors for your audience, because you have more "time" to connect with them on a deep, limbic level. Be sure readers can relate to your content enough to create those essential mental simulations.

Valuable Output — E-books are a unique opportunity to shine as The Mentor. Use their force wisely: Offer insight and advice that authentically helps your audience move through their Decision Journey. Don't try to sell them and your audience will receive your e-book as a valuable gift. And gifts are, as we've seen, the first step in reciprocity: a huge step in deepening relationships.

Giveaways

Just a quick note on giveaways, since they can be a fun way to bring the power of symbol into your relationships with your prospects and customers.

SALES SUPPORT TOOLS

Instead of the usual pens and monitor cleaners, have fun being creative in the freebies you give away. Look for things that could have symbolic meaning. One of my clients gives the gift of donating proceeds in the name of the client to Search and Rescue non-profits. That connection is symbolically related to how my client goes in and searches out hidden dollars that rescue the company.

Relevance doesn't have to be directly related to your product or service. I heard an interesting example about a sports clothing supplier for middle school kids. A key target audience was middle school coaches around the United States. This company built a free app that connected dates, locations, and weather, so coaches could get a heads up about the weather for their upcoming sports events. The app went viral. And sales shot through the roof. The app had nothing to do with sports clothing, but was of genuine value to the coaches.

But even if you can't come up with some "out of the box" freebie, go ahead and just give them a pen. I'm always amazed at how happy people are when I give them a pen in a gold cardboard box. It wasn't the cheapest pen — but also not the priciest. I think more than the pen, they love opening the box. It symbolizes a gift. Which, of course, stimulates reciprocity. And that's always a good thing.

TRY THIS:

Even though this chapter is called "Sales Support Tools," stay awake to the habit we all have of falling into "sales" mode.

This just happened today with a client. The Marketing Director sent me the first draft of an email blast to get my feedback. Yes, it was written in a wonderful, jargon-free, human voice that was refreshingly friendly and lively. But other than that, it was a perfectly normal, "state of the art" email. The message was self-focused, talking only about what was new with the company. There was nothing in there that the reader would find relevant or valuable. It had nothing in there that would be helpful to them in moving through their Decision Journey.

I understand. It is SO easy to fall back into creating self-focused content. Even I'm susceptible to it. It is a habit that's very hard to break. We have been trained — and that training has been reinforced year after year — to be self-focused in writing business communications. We're trained to talk about The Features and Advantages and Benefits. But that often has nothing to do with Value.

So, try this:

- Think of communications not as a way to make a sale, but as an opportunity to create a connection.

- Do whatever you can to remind yourself to be THEM-focused, to think of your audience FIRST.

Think what will be helpful to them *first*. THEN, tell them how you can help them get where they need to go.

- Before you do anything else, answer this question: **How can this piece be of value to the audience?** This is the most important first step in creating *every piece of communication*. Don't even start writing until you've figured that out. Try putting a Post-it note in a prominent place that says, "Where's the Value in What I'm About to Do?"

I understand, this can be really hard to do. Recently, I decided to write a blog post in response to an article in a prominent magazine that touted the top business communication trends. The tenets of The HERO Method — concepts I'd been talking about for years — were all there. The HERO Method was officially trending! But I couldn't write a blog about that…that is of no value to my audience. I had to somehow turn my impulse to create a chest-beating "I Told You So!" into a "Here's what's trending — here are my additional thoughts about them — and you can dive down into more information by linking to my previous articles on those topics." I'm here to tell you that was not easy to do. Because I was writing about The HERO Method and it's concepts, it took a lot of discipline to stay with The Value focus. To be honest, I'm not completely happy with the result. But if you're curious about reading the post, go to <u>TheHeroMethod.com/TheBook</u>.

CHAPTER 13

CREATING THE OUTPUT — SOCIAL MEDIA

Think of the most boring person you know. When you listen to them talk...you can't wait for them to stop. Chances are that person talks about himself or herself most of the time.

Well, just like any social encounter, social media is a potentially powerful platform that can be authentically connecting — or painfully boring. Rather than thinking of social media as a megaphone for what you want to say, think of social media as a listening platform.

To truly connect with others, human beings start by understanding the other person. We listen to their stories — to their problems, their hopes, their ideas. And in turn they do the same for us. Research has shown that sharing information about ourselves is intrinsically rewarding; sharing personal opinions activates the same brain circuitry as food and money.

Because of the potential for authentic dialogue, social media can play that essential connecting role unlike any other communication medium.

Having said that, Social Media isn't for everyone. There's nothing worse than an unattended social media site — with unanswered comments and old, outdated material. If you don't have the resources to focus on it and keep it alive and vibrant — and connecting — then I say don't do it at all. There's no shame in that. Don't look at social media as a "have to" in the marketing mix. But if your audience goes there, and IF you have the resources to keep it alive and connecting, go for it. If not, there are other ways to connect.

So assuming you've decided to go for the digital social sphere, here are some things to consider:

When customers go to a social media site with problems or suggestions, they usually just want to be heard. Even if it's a nasty complaint, letting them know they've been heard can be a powerful way to turn a negative into a positive. There are endless stories of customer dissatisfaction turning into enduring customer loyalty just by letting people know they've been heard.

But responding with a typically brusque, "Thank you for your input," will only leave them frustrated. Show your visitors that you hear them, even if you can't do anything about it right now. And if you say, "We'll get back to you on that" be sure to. Not following up will cause even more negativity.

As far as who writes your blog posts, hiring somebody to write for you can be a mistake if they're not authentically excited about blogging for you. A better idea is to find a few people in your company who are genuinely excited about blogging for you — and let them go for it.

The "create connection through emotion" rule we've been talking about throughout this book is as true here as anywhere. Content that gets the most likes and shares always evokes emotion. Content that gets shared a lot is also perceived as useful and is presented in a way that makes its easy to pass on. And a key element of content that has gone viral is that the products or ideas were presented with stories that people wanted to re-tell.

One of the powerful things about sharing experiences is that we have to create the story of that experience in our minds before we hit the "comment" button. That process sets the gist of the story into long-term memory. Quite simply, for humans to remember an experience, we must shape it into a story first. This is perhaps the main reason to use Social Media — to tell stories and let others tell similar stories right back.

This is also the reason to allow comments during webinars.

Social Media and Trust

We've previously explored how essential it is to build trust. It's the grand daddy of connection building.

But way too many companies fall on their face in their social media sites on this issue. Don't just act authentic; don't *try* to be authentic. (I think "authenticity" is on the verge of becoming just another buzzword in marketing).

To create trust, be real. Show your underbelly once in a while. To create trust, be a mentor who listens, not a one-sided know-it-all.

Create healthy social media rules. Do not allow bullying. Make your site a safe place to express ideas and opinions. By creating a safe place for visitors to express themselves, you'll create a place for positive emotional connection. But public flogging makes most people steer clear of expressing themselves — unless they're the kind of person who is always itching for a fight.

One of the saddest things about social media is that it has institutionalized public floggings. That's nothing less than disastrous for creating a connected community. I suggest clients try to gently re-train those people about appropriate social media skills — and if they can't be trained, exclude them from their sites.

SOCIAL MEDIA

TRY THIS:

- Letting people "like" your blog posts and webinars isn't just a social media construct. Every time we "like" something, a relationship with that company or person is forged in our brain. That's the neurological rationale for making sure people can "like" your stuff.

- Since storytelling sets experiences into long-term memory, encourage social media visitors and website attendees to share stories relevant to the topic.

- Institute a No Bullying policy on your social media sites. Encourage the expression and sharing of ideas without any personal bashing as a mask for disagreeing. Respectful disagreement is healthy. Foster the experience of being in a community of healthy, intelligent adults, where differing ideas are welcomed.

CHAPTER 14

CREATING THE OUTPUT — WHAT ABOUT FACTS?

We have been trained — and that training has been reinforced over the years — to assume that facts are necessary for clear communication.

We're worried about taking too long to say what we have to say. We think that copy has to be short. That nobody has the time to read long copy. And, facts can summarize points more succinctly than words and metaphors and story motifs.

But the fact is, people will spend the time to read well-constructed, compelling content. They do it all the time. They read articles and books. Why wouldn't they read your long copy if it was of value?

The only marketing that's directly measurable in terms of response and revenue is direct marketing. That was the field of my original training in marketing. The fact of the matter is: long copy works. It generates higher response rates than short copy. No exceptions. Remember that email that crashed the server? It was directed to IT decision-makers, and it was a two-page email.

Yes, it often feels like it would be easier to skip all the words and get right to the facts. I feel that. I really do. I'm tempted to do that all the time. But The HERO Method reminds me that every time I put out a fact, I'm disconnecting from my reader's emotional, limbic brain, shifting them to their logical, cortical brain — creating an emotional disconnection. So, IF I use facts, I use them sparingly and consciously — and am very quick to return to the limbic connection. I've practiced this on every page in this book.

Research shows over and over again that people shut down when faced with too many facts. They're not going to feel connected to you or your message — and they're not going remember what you've said.

What to do when you absolutely must include data

Once in a great while, you can't avoid facts. So here's what I suggest you do:

- **Facts need context to be remembered.** If you relay your facts within the context of something else — like a related mini-story or example — the audience is more likely to stay emotionally connected to you and is more likely to remember the facts.

- **Find the face behind the data.** See if you can tell a story about a human being that relates to the facts. This helps make the facts relevant because the audience can relate to the human being in the story. They will then associate the facts with that story. And *cha-ching!* The facts will be stored in retrievable long-term memory.

- **Leverage metaphors.** Association is the key to remembering even the most obscure facts. So, when you share data, find a metaphor that your audience can associate with it. If the metaphor relates to their everyday life, so much the better. For example, let's say you can relate your facts to an orange. Whenever your audience sees an orange, the orange will act as a trigger for the memory of that data.

- **Visual Analogies.** Creating a visual association to your data will lock the facts into your audience's memory. As an example, imagine you're creating a presentation on the population of elephants in Africa and Asia. Instead of numbers and locations on a chart, you can use small, medium, and large elephant icons on a map to represent three different ranges of population numbers and the regions where they're found. Creating visual simulations like this are tremendously powerful. Analogies are similar to metaphors in how they work in the brain. It's all about associating one thing with another — that's how the brain learns.

- **Use simple contrast.** Compare one thing to another in a way that highlights their differences. That's another great way to associate data in your audience's mind.

- **You probably don't need the data**. Dr. Brene Brown taught me this. Check out her TedTalks. She's a research professor who gave one of the most popular Ted Talks ever. Dr. Brown persuades effortlessly — always speaking from her authentic passion about her research. But she never once mentions her data.

CHAPTER 15

CREATING THE OUTPUT — NOW IT'S YOUR TURN

Here are what I hope will be helpful reminders that will prevent you from falling into old habits — and keep you out of that water-warming pot:

H — In every piece you create, you'll look to generate **H2H communications** instead of trying to sell, sell, sell.

- You'll remember that no business ever bought from another business.

- You'll always connect first on a human level.

- You'll always write in an authentic, human tone.

E — You'll write everything with the intention of creating authentic **emotional connections** from the very beginning.

- You'll remember that emotional resonance between you and your audience is essential.

- You'll remember that emotional connections are more persuasive than all the facts you can throw at them. And that trust is the most important emotion of all.

- You'll always make emotional connections first before you share facts or data. And you'll share those facts only if you have to…remembering that, chances are, you don't.

R — You'll always write about what is **relevant to your audience** based on who they are — and where they are in Their Decision Journey.

- You'll use the tools you learned here to create mental simulations in your audience's minds.

- You'll stay awake to the human tendency to be self-focused — and avoid it at all costs.

- You'll remember that you're <u>always</u> The Mentor offering helpful insight and advice, never forgetting who the real Hero is: Your Audience.

O — Before you begin to create any **Output**, you'll clearly see the need for the H and E and R.

- You'll strive to create communications that are <u>of value</u> to your audience.

- You'll freely use story motifs and archetypes, metaphors, and symbols to create mental simulations.

- You'll stay awake to any tendency to fall into "sales" mode.

Now that you've got new "3-D" glasses, and can look out at the world of communications from a new perspective, your content will never be the same!

If you'd like a handy hand-out that summarizes these thoughts, go to <u>TheHeroMethod.com/TheBook.</u>

EPILOGUE

> *"When planning a new picture, we don't think about grown-ups; we don't think about children. But just of that fine, clean, unspoiled spot deep down in every one of us that maybe the world has made us forget and maybe our pictures can help recall."*
> — WALT DISNEY

MY HOPE IS that you're now fired up to jump out of the frog-stewing pot and start exploring new ways to create connections with that unspoiled spot that's in every member of your audience. May you create authentic H2H connections with them at every phase of Their Decision Journey; may you give them something of value at every turn….and may everyone involved reap the rewards of your efforts.

I'd love to hear how you're using The HERO Method, or any questions you have about it. For more information, and some nice freebies, you can go to TheHeroMethod.com. Or reach out to me directly at Kathryn@TheHeroMethod.com.

Happy Hopping!

Kathryn Gillett

WITH GRATITUDE

I AM DEEPLY thankful for all my mentors, past and present, for their inspiration and support — without which the wondrous and unpredictable adventure of writing this book would never have started, nor finished. Unfortunately, there are too many of you to list individually here. So, for those of you still living, it will be my delight to thank each of you personally. And for those of you who have passed, you already know how indebted I am to you, because I've been sending my thanks to you all along.

AUTHOR'S NOTES

My training is in the scientific method, I'm a total research hound, and I'm one of those people who actually reads footnotes. But this book isn't a scientific treatise. It's a book that's exploring new concepts, new ways of looking at the way we communicate. So, even though I often refer to scientific research and other authors' works, I consciously chose not to create a book brimming with annotations. What I've done is included a bibliography of books I've read that relate to the subjects we're exploring here, and inserted a handful of citations in places where my esteemed reviewers felt they were needed. If you want to explore any of these concepts further, you have the bibliography to refer to. Or can always reach out to me.

BIBLIOGRAPHY

THE FOLLOWING ARE books and articles I read in preparation for writing this book, some of which are cited in its content. I'm not using the "accepted" format (which shouldn't be surprising at this point in the book). But what I have included is everything you'll need to find these resources for your further explorations. Enjoy the learning!

1. *A Whole New Mind: Why right-brainers will rule the future*, by Daniel H. Pink, 2006.

2. *All Marketers Tell Stories*, by Seth Godin, 2009.

3. *Bang! Getting your messages heard in a noisy world*, by Linda Kaplan Thaler and Robin Koval, 2005.

4. *Beyond Buzz: The next generation of world-of-mouth marketing*, by Lois Kelly, 2007.

5. *Buddha's Brain: The practical neuroscience of happiness, love, and wisdom*, by Rick Hanson with Richard Mendius, 2009.

6. *Building Trust in Business by Trusting*, by Dov Seidman, www.Businessweek.com, August 27 2009.

7. *Business Storytelling for Dummies*, by Karen Dietz and Lori L. Silverman, 2013.

8. *Buy-ology: Truth and lies about why we buy*, by Martin Lindstrom, 2008.

9. *Contagious: Why things catch on*, by Jonah Berger, 2013.

10. *Emotional Brain: The mysterious underpinnings of emotional life*, by Joseph LeDoux, 1996.

11. *Emotional Branding: The new paradigm for connecting brands to people*, by Marc Gobe, 2010.

12. *Good to Great: Why some companies make the leap…and others don't*, by Jim Collins, 2001.

13. *Gravitational Marketing: The science of attracting customers*, by Jimmy Vee, Travis Miller and Joel Bauer, 2015.

14. *How Customers Think: Essential insights into the mind of the market*, by Gerald Zaltman, 2013.

15. *How Does it Make You Feel? Why emotion wins the battle of the brands*, by Daryl Travis, Harrison Yates, 2013.

16. *How to Create Real relationships with Social Marketing*, by Ted Rubin, Mashable.com, June 18, 2012.

17. *Influence: The psychology of persuasion*, by Robert Cialdini, 2007.

18. *Invisible Ink*, by Brian McDonald, 2010.

19. *Lead with Story: A guide to crafting business narratives that captivate, convince and inspire*, by Paul Smith, 2012.

20. *Let my People Go Surfing: The education of a reluctant businessman*, by Yvon Chouinard, 2006.

21. *Marketers Have It Wrong: Forget engagement, consumers want simplicity*, by Patrick Spenner, Forbes.com, July 2, 2012.

22. *Marketing: A love story: How to matter to your customers*, by Bernadette Jiwa, 2013.

23. *On the Origins of Human Emotions: A sociological inquiry into the evolution of human affect*, by Jonathan Turner, 2000.

24. *Press Releases with Visuals Boost Views by Nearly Tenfold*, by Michael Sebastian, ragan.com, November 20, 2012.

25. *Ring of Power: A Jungian understanding of Wagner's Ring Cycle*, by Jean Shinoda Bolen, 2011.

26. *SCARF: A brain-based model for collaborating with and influencing others*, by David Rock, 2001.

27. *Secrets of Social Media Marketing: How to use online conversations and customer communities to turbo-charge your business*, by Paul Gillin, 2008.

28. *Selling the Invisible: A field guide to modern marketing*, by Harry Beckwith, 1999.

29. *SEO Isn't What You Think It Is*, by Veronica Fielding, FastCompany.com, August 10, 2012.

30. *Slow Ideas: Some innovations spread fast. How do you speed the ones that don't?*, by Atul Gawande, New Yorker, Annals of Medicine, 7/20/13.

31. *Story Proof: The science behind the startling power of story*, by Kendall Haven, 2011.

32. *Tell Me a Story*, by Diane Daniel, Ode Magazine, July/August 2012.

33. *Tell Me a Story: Narrative and intelligence*, by Roger C. Schank, 1995.

34. *The Corporate Web site is Dead, Long Live the New Corporate Web Site*, by Michele Mehl, GeekWire.com, 2013.

35. *The Creative Brain*, by Ned Herrmann, 1989.

36. *The Elements of Persuasion: The five key elements of stories that sell*, by Richard Maxwell and Robert Dickman, 2007.

37. *The Feeling of What Happens*, by Antonio Demasio, 2000.

38. *The Leader's Guide to Storytelling: Mastering the art and discipline of business narrative*, by Stephen Denning, 2011.

39. *The Mindful Brain*, by Daniel Siegel, 2007.

40. *The Origin of Stories*, by Brian Body, 2009.

41. *The Power of Storytelling*, by Jim Holtje, 2011.

42. *The Presentation Secrets of Steve Jobs: How to be insanely great in front of any audience*, by Carmine Gallo, 2009.

43. *The Rational Animal: How evolution made us smarter than we think*, by Douglas T. Kenrick and Vladas Griskevicius, 2013.

44. *The Righteous Mind: Why good people are divided by politics and religion*, by Jonathan Haidt, 2012.

45. *The Science of Trust*, by John M. Gottman, 2011.

46. *The Secret Language of Leadership: How leaders inspire action through narrative*, by Stephen Denning, 2007.

47. *The Secret Life of Metaphor: How metaphorical language inspires emotional insight and psychological change*, by James Geary, Ode Magazine, Spring 2011.

48. *The Speed of Trust*, by Stephen M. R. Covey, 2008.

49. *The Story Factor: Inspiration, influence and persuasion through the art of storytelling*, by Annette Simmons, 2009.

50. *The Storytelling Animal*, by Jonathan Gottschall, 2012.

51. *The Unbreakable Rules of Marketing*, by Cathey Armillas, 2012.

52. *The Zen of Selling: The way to profit from life's everyday lessons*, by Stan Adler, 2010.

53. *They Saw a Movie: Long-term memory for an extended audiovisual narrative*, by Orit Furman, Nimrod Dorfman, Uri Hasson, Lila Davachi, and Yadin, Dudai. Department of Neurobiology, The Weizmann Institute of Science.

54. *To Keep Your Customers, Keep it Simple*, by Patrick Spenner and Karen Freeman, Harvard Business Review, 2012.

55. *To Sell is Human: The surprising truth about moving others*, by Daniel H. Pink, 2012.

56. *Wake Me Up When the Data is Over: How organizations use story to drive results*, by Lori Silverman, 2006.

57. *What Americans Really Want*, by Frank Lutz, 2009.

58. *What Great Salespeople Do: The science of selling through emotional connection and the power of story*, by Michael Bosworth and Ben Zoldan, 2012.

59. *Whoever Tells the Best Story Wins: How to use your own stories to communicate with power and impact*, by Annette Simmons, 2015.

60. *Winning the Story Wars: Why those who tell — and live — the best stories will rule the future*, by Jonah Sachs, 2012.

61. *Wired for Story: The writer's guide to using brain science to hook readers from the very first sentence*, by Lisa Cron, 2012.

62. *Yes! 50 scientifically proven ways to be persuasive*, by Noah J. Goldstein and Steven J. Martin, 2008.

ABOUT THE AUTHOR

Kathryn Gillett is the creator of The HERO Method, a messaging and story strategist, and an award-winning writer. Some of the biggest names in global business — like Microsoft, Amazon, Dell, GE, and Philips — have relied on Kathryn to create messaging and content that inspires audiences to move themselves through The Decision

Journey. The fruits of her messages have been translated for distribution into more countries than are in the U.N.

After 30 years in marketing communications, Kathryn is recognized by many as an expert in her field. Various business associations have given her work awards of recognition, and she is a highly-rated and much-sought-after speaker.

Kathryn invites you to contact her at Kathryn@TheHeroMethod.com and to visit TheHeroMethod.com/TheBook.